Navigating Assessment and Collaboration with the Common Core State Standards

BOOK FOUR

Navigating Assessment and Collaboration with the Common Core State Standards

Larry Ainsworth | Derek C. Briggs
Maryann D. Wiggs | Laura Besser
Lisa Almeida

LEAD+
LEARN
PRESS

ENGLEWOOD, COLORADO

The Leadership and Learning Center
317 Inverness Way South, Suite 150
Englewood, Colorado 80112
Phone 1.866.399.6019 | Fax 303.504.9417
www.LeadandLearn.com

Published by Lead + Learn Press, a division of Houghton Mifflin Harcourt.

Library of Congress Cataloging-in-Publication Data

Ainsworth, Larry.
    Navigating assessment and collaboration with the common core state
standards / Larry Ainsworth, Derek C. Briggs, Maryann D. Wiggs, Laura Besser,
Lisa Almeida.
        pages cm. — (Getting ready for the common core handbook series ; BOOK
FOUR)
    Includes bibliographical references and index.
    ISBN 978-1-935588-17-7 (alk. paper)
    1. Education—Standards—United States. I. Title.
    LB3060.83.N494 2012
    379.1'580973—dc23

                                                                    2012001978

ISBN 978-1-935588-17-7

Printed in the United States of America

16 15 14 13 12   02 03 04 05 06 07 08

Contents

List of Exhibits

About the Authors

Larry Ainsworth is the Executive Director of Professional Development at The Leadership and Learning Center. He travels nationally and internationally to assist school systems in implementing best practices related to standards, assessment, and accountability across all grades and content areas. He is the author or coauthor of ten published books, including *Rigorous Curriculum Design, "Unwrapping" the Standards, Power Standards, Common Formative Assessments, Student Generated Rubrics,* and *Five Easy Steps to a Balanced Math Program.* Larry regularly works on-site in school systems to assist leaders and educators in understanding and implementing standards-based practices: prioritizing and "unwrapping" the standards, developing common formative assessments, designing authentic performance tasks, and creating rigorous curricular units of study in all content areas, pre-kindergarten through grade 12.

Derek C. Briggs is Associate Professor and Chair of the Research and Evaluation Methodology Program in the University of Colorado's School of Education. A psychometrican by training, he is a member of the technical advisory committees of three of the four large-scale assessment consortia that were funded under the Race to the Top Competition (NCSC, PARCC, and SBAC). His research agenda focuses upon building sound methodological approaches for the valid measurement and evaluation of growth in student achievement. Dr. Briggs is a member of the American Educational Research Association, the National Council for Measurement in Education, and the Psychometric Society. Some of his notable publications include "Due diligence and the evaluation of teachers: A review of the value-added analysis underlying the effectiveness rankings of Los Angeles Unified School District teachers by the Los Angeles Times" (National Education Policy Center); "Preparation for college admissions exams" (Report Commissioned by the National Association of College Admissions Counselors); "The impact of vertical scaling decisions on growth interpretations" (*Educational Measurement: Issues and Practice*); "Diagnostic Assessment with Ordered Multiple-Choice Items" (*Educational Assessment*); and "Generalizability in item response modeling" (*Journal of Educational Measurement*).

With more than four decades of experience in education, **Maryann D. Wiggs** brings an abundance of expertise and wisdom to her presentations, ensuring that teachers and administrators gain practical strategies for enhancing instructional performance. As the former Assistant Superintendent of Curriculum and Instruction and Executive Director of Learning Services in two Colorado school districts, Maryann has been instrumental in orchestrating the alignment of all aspects of the leaders' and teachers' work to improve the quality of instruction in the classroom, including alignment of standards, assessment, curriculum, instruction, interventions, supervision, and evaluation. Maryann is a former speech pathologist, special and general education teacher, behavior consultant, and teacher leader, having served learners at the elementary, middle, high school, and college levels.

Laura Besser is a Professional Development Associate and Director of Content with The Leadership and Learning Center. She is an instructional leader who combines powerful research and best practices in her approach to helping educators. Laura provides professional development support, and her expertise in standards, assessment, data analysis, instruction, and leadership results in high-quality professional learning. Laura was a pioneer in the Data Teams process, and as a building principal she saw dramatic gains in teaching and learning as a result of using the Data Teams model. Laura is a contributing author of *Data Teams: The Big Picture* and coauthor of *Leaders Make It Happen: An Administrator's Guide to Data Teams.*

Lisa Almeida is the Director of Certification and a Distinguished Professional Development Associate with The Leadership and Learning Center. Lisa has vast experiences as an educator and wears dual hats with The Center, which enables her to continue to work with practitioners. Lisa supports clients and their certified trainers with much of The Center's core work that includes, but is not limited to, Authentic Performance Tasks: The Engaging Classroom Assessments, Decision Making for Results and Data Teams, Common Formative Assessments, certification trainings, and implementation support. Prior to her work with The Center, Lisa was a client of The Center's. As a district administrator, Lisa supported colleagues in the implementation of Priority Standards, performance assessments and data-driven decision making. Lisa's dedication and contribution to education is nonstop. In addition to supporting The Center's clients, she is a contributing author to a variety of publications, including *Standards and Assessment: The Core of Quality Instruction, Ahead of the Curve: The Power of Assessment to Transform Teaching and Learning*, and *Eliminating Achievement Gaps by Meeting the Needs of the Whole Child.*

Introduction

The Leadership and Learning Center is pleased to share with readers this capstone handbook in the series on *Getting Ready for the Common Core*. Handbooks, by design, are practical guides for "doing it yourself" and for rechecking your work and "doing over" things that can be improved upon. This fourth handbook, *Navigating Assessment and Collaboration with the Common Core State Standards*, focuses on using formative assessment processes with the Common Core, as well as strategies for aligning Professional Learning Community and Data Team practices as continuous improvement structures ensuring sustainability. Once again, as experts committed to improving education across the United States, Professional Development Associates from The Center gathered together to create this handbook in order to serve as a "guide on the side" for leaders and teachers embarking on the call to action in implementing the rigorous expectations outlined in the English language arts and mathematics Common Core State Standards (CCSS).

In Chapter One, author Larry Ainsworth starts us off on the final segment of our journey by providing the rationale and research for using common formative assessment to assess progress when implementing the Common Core State Standards. The reader is provided with step-by-step instructions, complete with examples, for the 10-step process for developing common formative assessments. The chapter concludes with practical suggestions for including teachers in the process of developing common formative assessments.

In Chapter Two, author Lisa Almeida provides the rationale for "unwrapping" the standards—one of the most powerful practices for fully getting to know the concepts and skills embedded in the Common Core State Standards. This is a practical, hands-on chapter that every educator must read in order to begin the foundational work for instructional planning and assessment development. Step-by-step instructions, with examples, are provided. The author concludes with specific strategies for how to get started.

In Chapter Three, author Laura Besser highlights the marriage of three practices: data, collaboration, and the Common Core State Standards. The author advises that when each is used separately, educators may see some results, but when the practices are effectively used together, educators can expect amazing gains in teaching, learning, and leadership. This chapter outlines the powerful practices used in Professional Learning Communities and Data Teams as high-leverage strategies to help deliver the hope and promise of the CCSS and make educational transformation a reality. This chapter clearly spells out explicit practices in a continuous improvement model for implementing the CCSS.

On the journey to *Navigating Assessment and Collaboration with the Common Core State Standards*, readers will find Chapter Four, authored by Maryann Wiggs, to be a junction in the road. This chapter on using feedback and formative assessment to advance learning synthesizes information gleaned from the first three chapters on using common formative assessment, "unwrapping" the standards, and leveraging Professional Learning Communities and Data Teams as continuous improvement structures.

The power of effective feedback is at the heart of each chapter in this book, weaving a tapestry of powerful practices to advance learning along the pathways articulated in the Common Core State Standards.

In Chapter Five, "Looking Ahead to Large-Scale Assessment of the Common Core State Standards," author Derek Briggs provides an overview of what it means for the nation's students to step up to the 2014–2015 challenge and demonstrate success on novel and innovative next-generation assessments. In this final chapter, the author outlines the components of two large-scale assessment consortia—the Partnership for Assessment of Readiness for College and Careers (PARCC) and the SMARTER Balanced Assessment Consortium (SBAC). He describes the approach known as evidence-centered design that both consortia are using to build their testing blueprints. Readers are provided with a glimpse of how these new assessments will provide greater emphasis on complex thinking as evidenced by student responses to performance-based tasks and technology-enhanced items.

Each handbook on *Getting Ready for the Common Core* focuses on a unifying theme to provide leaders and educators with the rationale and tools for navigating the terrain of implementing the CCSS. The first handbook in this series provided guidance for leaders by examining the leadership aspects of creating a rigorous school culture in which all students can thrive in demonstrating proficiency of the Common Core State Standards. The second handbook provided specific strategies for navigating the English language arts CCSS, while the third handbook provided explicit guidance for navigating the mathematics CCSS. It is The Leadership and Learning Center's hope that educators will continue to revisit each of these handbooks and use them as guides to implementing the Common Core in a way that will enable all students to succeed in their educational pursuits, their careers, and their lives.

> *What we call the beginning is often the end*
> *And to make an end is to make a beginning.*
> *The end is where we start from.*
>   —T. S. Eliot (*Four Quartets*, 1943)

While this fourth handbook signals the end of this series on understanding and navigating the Common Core State Standards, it represents merely the beginning, the starting point, of the arduous journey of actually implementing these rigorous standards in classrooms throughout the country. Let us begin that journey now.

MARYANN D. WIGGS, 2012
Colorado Springs, Colorado

Connecting Common Core State Standards with Common Formative Assessments

Larry Ainsworth

The Common Core State Standards Initiative (CCSSI) has made educational history. Forty-six states and the District of Columbia have voluntarily adopted the Common Core since its official launch in 2010. This fact presents a number of interesting challenges for educators and leaders to face, now and in the very near future. Among them:

- How to help educators "get to know" these new, more rigorous standards and begin implementing them in the classroom.

- How to redesign curricula, instruction, and in-school assessments to align with the CCSS.

- How to "bridge the rigor gap" between the CCSS and existing district and state assessments.

- How to prepare students for success on national assessments aligned to the CCSS when they are first administered in 2014–15.

It is going to take careful planning on the part of school and district leaders and educators to merge the CCSS with the standards and assessment processes they have already spent years developing. But as challenging as this may seem, it *can* be done. The important message is this: *Don't wait to implement these new standards.* Create a multiyear action plan to have educators and students ready for the 2014–15 assessments now being developed by the SMARTER Balanced Assessment Consortium (SBAC) and Partnership for Assessment of Readiness for College and Careers (PARCC). Then implement that action plan in doable steps each year.

In this chapter, I will suggest practical steps educators and leaders can take to use proven, standards-based practices and common formative assessments (CFAs) to gauge students' understanding of the English language arts and mathematics CCSS. However, keep in mind that these strategies are equally applicable to all other content areas that will continue to focus on state standards. By using formative assessment results *diagnostically*, educators can differentiate instruction as needed to help all students improve their performance on current school, district, and state assessments aligned to state standards, and eventually on the national assessments that will be directly aligned to the CCSS.

CONNECTING STANDARDS, ASSESSMENT, CURRICULUM, AND INSTRUCTION

Because standards, assessments, curriculum, and instruction must work together like synchronized gears, it is important to address all four topics in relation to the Common Core State Standards *simultaneously*.

Standards are the "what"—the academic learning outcomes

that each student needs to know and be able to do in each grade and course. Because the *number* of K–12 grade-specific standards in the English language arts CCSS is so high, and because the *rigor* in the fewer mathematics CCSS is so great, the need to classify these standards as being either Priority or supporting is critical. Most educators are not going to have sufficient classroom instruction time during each school year to teach, assess, reteach, and reassess their students on *all* of these new standards with an equal degree of emphasis. *Prioritizing* the CCSS—without *eliminating* any standards or "breaking" the vertical learning progressions inherent in their design—will do much to help educators focus both instruction and assessment and send their students forward with these standards as "assured competencies," prepared for the next level of learning.

However, the CCSS by themselves—even when prioritized—are not enough. "To be effective in improving education and getting all students ready for college, workforce training, and life, the [Common Core State] Standards must be partnered with a content-rich curriculum and robust assessments, both aligned to the standards" (CCSSI, 2010b).

Curriculum should serve as both the detailed road map and the high-quality delivery system for ensuring that all students achieve the desired end: the attainment of their designated grade- or course-specific standards within *any* particular content area. A rigorous curriculum must provide educators with an inclusive set of intentionally aligned components—clearly understood grade-specific standards with matching assessments, high-quality lessons with authentic performance tasks, and research-based instructional strategies—organized into sequenced units of study for each grade level and course. A *unit of study* is a series of specific lessons, learning experiences, and related assessments—based on designated Priority Standards and related supporting standards—for a topical, skills-based, or thematic focus that may last anywhere from two to six weeks (Ainsworth, 2010).

Assessments (pre-assessments, progress-monitoring checks and post-assessments) should provide the evidence of whether or not students are achieving the goal and purpose of the curriculum: the attainment of the Priority and supporting standards foundational to each unit of study. A powerful method that educators can use to pinpoint the precise concepts and skills contained in the wording of the standards assigned to each unit is to "unwrap" those standards (Ainsworth, 2003). In this context, to "unwrap" means to analyze and deconstruct each standard in focus to determine exactly what students need to know (teachable concepts) and be able to do (skills). Educators then design assessment questions *directly matched* to the "unwrapped" concepts, skills, and levels of thinking skill rigor. Student responses to those assessment questions will produce valid and reliable evidence as to the degree of student understanding relative to those specific concepts and skills. (Refer to Bloom's Revised Taxonomy [Anderson and Krathwohl, 2001] or Webb's Depth of Knowledge [Webb, 1997].)

Instruction is the "how." Specialized instructional strategies provide the means educators use to help students learn the standards and then demonstrate their understanding on a variety of informal and formal assessments. However, instructional planning should *follow*, not lead, the entire unit design process, as indicated in this design sequence: First, select and "unwrap" the particular Priority Standards identified as the focus for a unit of study. Next, create the end-of-unit assessment directly aligned to those "unwrapped" standards and levels of thinking skill rigor. Then, design the unit based on the knowledge and skills students will need to know and be able to demonstrate on the end-of-unit assessment. Finally, plan instruction and the sequence of learning progressions ("building block" segments of instruction) to implement the unit lessons, activities, and student learning experiences. While teaching the unit of study, create short, informal progress-monitoring checks aligned to the end-of-unit assessment. Administer these quick checks for understanding to coincide with learning progressions (i.e., after each important "chunk" of unit instruction, determine student understanding of that instructional segment with a short informal assessment). *Use* the results to carefully diagnose individual student learning needs and plan accordingly for differentiation, intervention, and/or enrichment. In this way, assessment results can truly inform instruction.

USING ASSESSMENT RESULTS TO INFORM INSTRUCTION

The one true purpose of educational assessment is to correctly determine student understanding of the standards in focus and then to use those assessment results to inform, modify, adjust, enrich, and differentiate instruction to meet the learning needs of all students. Here is what W. James Popham has to say about the essential purpose of instructional assessment:

> Teachers use test (results) in order to make inferences about their students' cognitive status. Once those score-based inferences have been made, the teacher then reaches instructional decisions based (at least in part) on those inferences. *Educational assessment revolves around inference making.* (Popham, 2003, p. 60, emphasis added)

It is essential for educators to understand that the primary reason for assessing their students and then analyzing the assessment results is to accurately infer what students need next in terms of their learning. The following six sequential steps for using assessment results to inform instructional decision making, from *Rigorous Curriculum Design,* have proven very helpful to educators (Ainsworth, 2010, pp. 137–138):

1. **Know your purpose.** All of the assessment literature points to this underlying first step in planning assessments. Determine exactly what it is you want to find out, what it is you want the assessment to do, and why you are administering the assessment in the first place.

2. **Determine the appropriate assessment that will accomplish your identified purpose.** In this context, "appropriate" means the specific format(s) most likely to tell you what you want to know. The major assessment formats and their related types include: *selected-response* (multiple-choice, true/false, matching, fill-in using a provided word bank), *constructed-response* (short or extended writing), and *performance-based* (physical demonstration). Note: Performance-based assessments are typically more appropriate for performance-based content areas, for very young children who are not yet taking written assessments, and for students with special learning needs.

3. **Select or create a quality assessment.** Take great care in choosing questions from an external source and/or crafting the assessment questions, either by yourself (if you are the only educator teaching a specific grade or

course) or with grade-level or course colleagues. If a question is faulty in any way, and students answer it incorrectly, you will later have to determine whether the question itself was the problem or whether students simply did not know the content upon which it was based. When completing this step, refer to published guidelines for selecting or creating quality selected- and constructed-response questions. (The Leadership and Learning Center's Common Formative Assessments seminar manual provides such guidelines.)

4. **Administer and score the assessment; analyze the assessment results.** Look for evidence of student learning, specific to your purpose, in the student responses. Conduct an item analysis, determining which questions individual students answered correctly and which ones they did not.

5. **Make an *accurate* inference.** This will be possible only if the assessment questions that you selected or created in step 3 are of quality and provide valid and reliable data. If the questions *are* well written and yet students are responding in error, identify the conceptual misunderstandings students are having.

6. **Reflect and adjust instructional decisions *in a timely manner*.** Timely feedback is necessary if the assessment results are to be used formatively. Determine instructional "next steps" for students based on the inferences you have made, and select the appropriate instructional strategies accordingly.

COMMON ASSESSMENTS—
FORMATIVE AND SUMMATIVE

A common *formative* assessment (CFA) is an "in-process" assessment *for* learning based on the "unwrapped" Priority Standards for a unit of study. Grade-alike and course-alike educators collaboratively create and administer a pre-CFA and a post-CFA to all of their students at the beginning and end of each unit. The educators use the *pre*-CFA results to set learning goals for their students, select appropriate instructional strategies, and plan how to differentiate instruction based on what individual students currently know and are able to do. The *post*-CFA serves as the end-of-unit test. Educators again score student work, analyze the results, make accurate inferences, and determine what students need next instructionally. Then, during a "buffer" period of one to five days prior to beginning the next unit, they use the *post*-CFA results to reteach and reassess students who are not yet proficient. They enrich and extend the understanding of those students who *are* proficient. Student results can be graded and recorded either before or after the "buffer" period.

Another type of common assessment is the common *summative* assessment (CSA), also collaboratively created and administered by grade-level or course-alike colleagues as the culminating or final assessment *of* learning administered at the end of a unit of study, quarter, trimester, grade, and/or entire course of study. Educators using a CSA at the close of a unit of study will also administer a pre- and post-CFA during the unit. What differs is that they will administer the post-CFA *a few days before* the scheduled finish of the unit. They will then use the post-CFA results to continue differentiating instruction for students prior to administering the end-of-unit CSA. Using this assessment approach, the "buffer" period occurs *before* students take the CSA, which is then graded and recorded as a summative measure.

When intentionally aligned to summative assessments *of* learning (whether school-, district-, or state-based), common formative assessments *for* learning provide educators with predictive value as to how students are likely to perform on those summative assessment measures *in time* for them to "change up" instruction as needed. This intentional alignment includes the particular standards being assessed, the levels of rigor, the academic language, and the different types of question formats students will encounter on state and national assessments.

After summarizing a body of research on the impact of formative assessments, distilled from 4,000 studies spanning 40 years, Dylan Wiliam concluded that "When well-implemented, formative assessments can effectively *double* the speed of student learning" (Wiliam, 2008, p. 36).

Note the beginning phrase of Wiliam's quote: "When well-implemented." It is not enough just to *administer* formative assessments. To realize their full potential for improving student achievement, such assessments must be carefully constructed, student results must be thoughtfully analyzed, inferences must be accurately made, and subsequent instruction must be differentiated to meet student learning needs accordingly. This applies equally to *summative* assessments. The results of well-constructed assessments of learning can also be used *formatively* by educators if they will analyze those results to diagnose individual student learning needs and modify instruction, either the next day or in the next unit of study.

Common formative assessments provide "snapshots" of student understanding of each unit's Priority Standards *only*. Together with informal classroom assessments and student work products based on the unit's Priority Standards *and* supporting standards, these various kinds of assessments produce a "photo album" of student understanding.

Keeping this foundational understanding in mind, let us now look at how to apply these ideas to the design of a quality common formative post-assessment based on certain priority Common Core standards selected for a unit of study.

HOW TO DESIGN A QUALITY CFA BASED ON COMMON CORE PRIORITY STANDARDS

The 10-step process I created for The Leadership and Learning Center's Common Formative Assessments seminar shows educators and leaders how to construct a CFA that includes a blend of selected- and constructed-response questions with accompanying scoring guides. These steps, illustrated with an accompanying Grade 6 English language arts CCSS example, are as follows:

Step 1: Choose a focus for the unit of study

Step 2: Identify matching priority CCSS

Step 3: "Unwrap" the priority CCSS

Step 4: Create a graphic organizer

Step 5: Determine the Big Ideas

Step 6: Write the Essential Questions

Step 7: Write selected-response items

Step 8: Write constructed-response items (short and/or extended)

Step 9: Create scoring guides for constructed-response items

Step 10: Write Essential Question and Big Idea directions

Step 1: Choose a Focus for the Unit of Study

The name of the Grade 6 sample unit of study is "Interdisciplinary Informational Text," and it is scheduled for about four weeks of instruction. The primary focus will be on literacy skills applied to social studies content. (Note: Math educators referencing the math CCSS can follow the exact same process illustrated here.)

Step 2: Identify Matching Priority CCSS

The following four priority CCSS in English language arts match the focus of the unit. Even though supporting CCSS and specific social studies content standards will also be taught and assessed during the unit, the CFA will be based *only* on the targeted Priority Standards shown here.

CCSS Reading Standards for Informational Text 6–12:
RI.6.2: Determine a central idea of a text and how it is conveyed through particular details; provide a summary of the text distinct from personal opinions or judgments.
RI.6.6: Determine an author's point of view or purpose in a text and explain how it is conveyed in the text.

CCSS Reading Standards for Literacy in History/Social Studies 6–12:
RH.6–8.8: Distinguish among fact, opinion, and reasoned judgment in a text.

CCSS Writing Standards 6–12:

W.6.2: Write informative/explanatory texts to examine a topic and convey ideas, concepts, and information through the selection, organization, and analysis of relevant content.

Step 3: "Unwrap" the Priority CCSS

To "unwrap" the standards means to identify the teachable concepts that students need to *know* and the skills they need to be able to *do* in the wording of the standards. To do this, underline the important nouns and noun phrases, and circle or capitalize the verbs. Even though the initial task of "unwrapping" is to separate concepts from skills, the two remain interrelated, as will be shown in steps 4 and 5.

RI.6.2: DETERMINE a central idea of a text and how it is conveyed through particular details; PROVIDE a summary of the text distinct from personal opinions or judgments.

RI.6.6: DETERMINE an author's point of view or purpose in a text and EXPLAIN how it is conveyed in the text.

RH.6–8.8: DISTINGUISH among fact, opinion, and reasoned judgment in a text.

W.6.2: WRITE informative/explanatory texts to EXAMINE a topic and CONVEY ideas, concepts, and information through the selection, organization, and analysis of relevant content.

Step 4: Create a Graphic Organizer

Prepare a graphic organizer (outline, bulleted list, concept map, or chart) that represents the underlined concepts, the circled (or capitalized) skills, and the *approximate* level of thinking skill rigor, as indicated by Bloom's Revised Taxonomy (Anderson and Krathwohl, 2001) or by Webb's Depth of Knowledge (Webb, 1997), a needed resource for this step. How each skill is applied to a particular concept determines its corresponding level of cognitive rigor. Determining the level of rigor in each skill is an important factor when later designing assessment questions and instruction to reflect that same degree of rigor.

Note in the step 4 example, Exhibit 1.1, the *addition* of verbs that more accurately represent the thinking skills needed to carry out the given skill. In the first example: to DETERMINE the central idea through details, one is actually required to ANALYZE, EVALUATE, and SUPPORT ideas. This helps to determine the approximate cognitive level(s) and explains the additional cognitive skill numbers listed in the third column.

Step 5: Determine the Big Ideas

"Big ideas" represent the three or four foundational understandings—main ideas, conclusions, or generalizations relative to the unit's "unwrapped" concepts—that educators want their students to discover and state in their own words by the end of the unit of study. Written as complete sentences (not phrases), Big Ideas convey to students the benefit or value of learning the standards in focus. They represent what educators want students to remember long after instruction ends. These foundational understandings

BOOK FOUR
EXHIBIT
1.1

Graphic Organizer of "Unwrapped" Concepts and Skills

"Unwrapped" Concepts (What students need to know)	"Unwrapped" Skills (What students need to be able to do)	Bloom's Taxonomy Levels

• central idea
  • conveyed through
    • details
    • relevant content
• summary
  • distinct from personal opinions/judgments
• author's point of view
• author's purpose
• fact
• opinion
• reasoned judgment
• informative writing
• expository text
	• **DETERMINE** (central idea *through details*)—ANALYZE, EVALUATE, SUPPORT	2, 4, 5

	• **PROVIDE** (summary without personal opinions/judgments)	2
	• **DETERMINE** (author's point of view)—ANALYZE, INFER	4
	• **DETERMINE** (author's purpose)	2
	• **EXPLAIN** (how it is conveyed)	2
	• **DISTINGUISH** (fact/opinion/reasoned judgment)	2
	• **WRITE** (informative/explanatory texts)	6
	• **EXAMINE** (topic)—ANALYZE	4
	• **CONVEY** (ideas/concepts/information through selection/organization/analysis of relevant content)	4, 5

can be **broad** ("People can justify their conclusions with data"; applicable to several content areas), **topical** ("The position of a digit determines its value"; applicable to math only), or **both** ("Objects can be compared and classified by their different attributes"; applicable to math and science). Big ideas—whether broad, topical, or both—help students scaffold their understanding so they can eventually make further generalizations and connections to other units of study within a discipline and to other disciplines.

Here are three suggested Big Ideas for this unit of study, derived from the "unwrapped" concepts:

1. You can convey or explain a central idea by providing details and relevant content.

2. An effective summary of informational text is free of personal opinions and judgments.

3. An author of informational text tries to convey a particular point of view through relevant facts and without bias.

Step 6: Write the Essential Questions

"Essential Questions" are engaging, open-ended questions that educators use to spark student interest in learning the content of the unit about to commence. Even though plainly worded (and hopefully engaging for students), they carry with them an underlying rigor. Responding to them in a way that demonstrates genuine understanding requires more than superficial thought. Along with the "unwrapped" concepts and skills from the Priority Standards, educators use the Essential Questions throughout the unit to sharply focus instruction and assessment. At the beginning of a unit of study, educators post, in a prominent location in the classroom or instructional space, two to four questions written in bold, colorful lettering. They explain to their students that these questions are a special type of question known as an "Essential Question," and that by the end of the unit of study, they want all students to be able to respond to each of these Essential Questions with a corresponding "Big Idea" stated in their own words.

Exhibit 1.2 shows the Essential Questions for this unit of study, with the corresponding Big Ideas placed side-by-side to show how the Big Ideas are the intended student responses to the Essential Questions.

Essential Questions and Corresponding Big Ideas

Essential Questions	Corresponding Big Ideas
1. How can you convey a central idea when writing informative or expository texts?	1. You can convey or explain a central idea by providing details and relevant content.
2. What makes a summary of informational text effective?	2. An effective summary of informational text is free of personal opinions and judgments.
3. How does an author of informational text convey a particular point of view?	3. An author of informational text tries to convey a particular point of view through relevant facts and without bias.

Step 7: Write Selected-Response Items

For the selected-response section of the CFA, students will first read a provided social studies passage about Marco Polo (not included here) and then answer four related multiple-choice questions, one of which is shown here for illustration. The directions for writing selected-response questions appear in Exhibit 1.3. Note the emphasis on matching the rigor of the question to the rigor of the "unwrapped" skills. For this reason, the "unwrapped" skills, concepts, and thinking skill levels are first copied from the graphic organizer and recorded above the questions. This aids educators in designing questions at the appropriate level of difficulty. The one sample question shown here reflects *three* of the "unwrapped" concepts, skills, and levels of rigor (shown in bold print). The completed assessment (including both selected- and constructed-response questions) will address *all* of the targeted skills, concepts, and thinking skill levels.

BOOK FOUR
EXHIBIT
1.3

Writing Selected-Response Questions

Selected-Response
(Multiple-Choice, Matching, True-False, Select from Provided Word List)

Directions:

1. Copy *all* of the "unwrapped" skills, related concepts, and matching Bloom's levels.
2. **Bold** those you will assess through the selected-response format.
3. Write assessment questions that *directly match* the approximate level of rigor for each skill.
4. Make all distracters (incorrect answer choices) plausible and/or reflective of common student errors or misconceptions.

(2, 4, 5) DETERMINE (central idea *through details*)—ANALYZE, EVALUATE, SUPPORT
(2) PROVIDE (summary without personal opinions/judgments)
(4) DETERMINE (author's point of view)—ANALYZE, INFER
(2) DETERMINE (author's purpose)
(2) EXPLAIN (how it is conveyed)
(2) DISTINGUISH (fact/opinion/ reasoned judgment)
(6) WRITE (informative/explanatory texts)
(4) EXAMINE (topic)—ANALYZE
(4, 5) CONVEY (ideas/concepts/information through selection/organization/analysis of relevant content)

Note how the bolded skills and Bloom's levels are represented in the following sample question:

1. Which of these is a **summary** of the section called "Marco Milione"?
(Levels 2, 4, 5) *

A. Marco Polo was disliked because he wrote about other cultures that were more advanced.

B. Marco Polo made up all the stories about different countries in his book, *The Travels of Marco Polo.*

C. Europeans did not believe Marco Polo's claim that the Chinese had paper money and books.

D. *The Travels of Marco Polo* told about things Europeans had never seen, so many thought Marco Polo made up the stories.

* Source: Minnesota Department of Education.

When creating the answer choices for a selected-response question, first write the correct answer and then write the distracters (incorrect answer choices) so they are *all* plausible and/or reflect common student errors or misconceptions. Plausible means the distracters are all believable in the context of the question; there should be no easy elimination by students of humorous or "out-in-left-field" choices. Including common student errors and misconceptions as distracters will assist educators in pinpointing where and why students are having trouble understanding certain concepts or skills. Writing the distracters with these key points in mind will increase the overall rigor of the assessment questions.

Because the assessment questions will be designed *before* unit instruction begins, the level of rigor in the assessment questions will signal the need for a matching level of related instruction and a corresponding level of student thinking necessary to answer the questions correctly. For example, if the "unwrapped" skill and related concept in focus is "INTERPRET implied information," a level-four skill in Bloom's Taxonomy, the assessment question must be written as an *inference* question, not a lower-level recall question, since students will need to demonstrate their ability to *infer* information from the text. The related classroom instruction during the unit must then enable students to practice this higher-level skill so they can respond correctly to its related question(s) on the end-of-unit assessment.

Step 8: Write Constructed-Response Items (Short and/or Extended)

Student understanding of certain "unwrapped" concepts and skills can be more appropriately assessed in the constructed-

BOOK FOUR EXHIBIT 1.4

Writing Short Answer Constructed-Response Questions

Constructed-Response
(Short Answer)

Directions:
1. Copy **all** of the "unwrapped" skills, related concepts, and matching Bloom's levels.
2. **Bold** those you will assess through the short answer constructed-response format.
3. Write assessment questions that **directly match** the approximate level of rigor for each skill.

(2, 4, 5) DETERMINE (central idea *through details*)—ANALYZE, EVALUATE, SUPPORT
(2) PROVIDE (summary without personal opinions/judgments)
(4) DETERMINE (author's point of view)—ANALYZE, INFER
(2) DETERMINE (author's purpose)
(2) EXPLAIN (how it is conveyed)
(2) DISTINGUISH (fact/opinion/reasoned judgment)
(6) WRITE (informative/explanatory texts)
(4) EXAMINE (topic)—ANALYZE
(4, 5) CONVEY (ideas/concepts/ information through selection/organization/analysis of relevant content)

**Again, note how the different bolded skills and Bloom's
levels are represented in the following sample short
constructed-response question:**

Directions: In the section of the article "Marco Milione," which of Marco's stories do you think would have been most difficult for Europeans to believe? Give a reason from the article to support your answer. Give your own reason(s) why that story would have been more difficult for people to believe than the other ones. Your responses will be evaluated using the "Constructed-Response Short Answer Scoring Guide" (shown in Exhibit 1.5). **(Levels 2, 4, 5, 6)**

response format as opposed to the selected-response format. To make a *more accurate inference* regarding student understanding, include on the CFA a blend of selected-response *and* constructed-response (short and/or extended) questions. For example, in the short constructed-response question in Exhibit 1.4, two of the bold-print skills in particular (write, convey) lend themselves more effectively to students' *written* responses.

Step 9: Create Scoring Guides for Constructed-Response Items

Used in conjunction with constructed-response written assessments (and performance-based assessments), the scoring guide is a written set of specific criteria describing different levels of student proficiency relative to those assessments. Avoid the vague and highly subjective language typically used to describe performance levels on rubrics. Words like "some, few, many, most, little, generally, clearly, elaborately, appropriately" and so on, can be interpreted in multiple ways, making it difficult—and time-consuming—for educators to be able to individually decide or collaboratively agree upon an accurate score for a student's work. Specificity in wording and format on a scoring guide is critical. Without it, there can be no reliability in terms of the scoring guide's consistency. When creating the scoring guide, a key point to remember is to directly match the scoring guide criteria to the task directions. For example, if the task states, "In your answer, you must provide two or more supporting details," then the scoring guide needs to include the same requirement: "Provides two or more supporting details." The scoring guide format presented here can be used effectively with both short-response and

BOOK FOUR EXHIBIT 1.5

Creating a Scoring Guide for Short Answer Constructed-Response Questions

Constructed-Response
Short Answer Scoring Guide

Goal
- ☐ Identifies personal choice of story most difficult for Europeans to believe
- ☐ Supports choice with supporting detail(s) from article
- ☐ Gives own reason(s) why that story is most difficult to believe

Progressing
- ☐ Meets two of the "Goal" criteria

Beginning
- ☐ Meets fewer than two of the "Goal" criteria
- ☐ Task to be repeated after reteaching
- ☐ Comments:

extended-response questions. Educators across the United States have enthusiastically endorsed this time-saving, user-friendly approach to designing rubrics.

Note: Because short-answer assessment questions are usually quickly scored as being correct, partially correct, or incorrect, there are only three performance levels in the example in Exhibit 1.5. Educators can certainly add an "advanced" level if they wish.

Steps 8 and 9: Constructed-Response (Extended) with Accompanying Scoring Guide.

Shown in Exhibit 1.6 is the extended-response question included on the CFA for this particular unit of study. Note how *all* of the

BOOK
FOUR
EXHIBIT
1.6

Writing Extended Answer Constructed-Response Questions

Constructed-Response
(Extended Answer)

Directions:
1. Copy *all* of the "unwrapped" skills, related concepts, and matching Bloom's levels.
2. **Bold** those you will assess through the extended-response format.
3. Write assessment questions that *directly match* the approximate level of rigor for each skill.

(2, 4, 5) DETERMINE (central idea *through details*)—ANALYZE, EVALUATE, SUPPORT
(2) PROVIDE (summary without personal opinions/judgments)
(4) DETERMINE (author's point of view)—ANALYZE, INFER
(2) DETERMINE (author's purpose)
(2) EXPLAIN (how it is conveyed)
(2) DISTINGUISH (fact/opinion/ reasoned judgment)
(6) WRITE (informative/explanatory texts)
(4) EXAMINE (topic)—ANALYZE
(4, 5) CONVEY (ideas/concepts/ information through
election/organization/analysis of relevant content)

Note how this two-part extended-response question addresses *all* of the bolded Priority Standards concepts, skills, and Bloom's levels that are the focus of this particular unit of study.

Directions: Respond to *both* parts of the following. You may answer each part separately or both parts together. Make sure you include an answer for *each* question that appears in both parts. Your responses will be evaluated using the "Constructed-Response Extended Answer Scoring Guide" (shown in Exhibit 1.7).

Part 1: Write a short *summary* of "Marco Polo and the 'Million Lies'" without adding your *personal opinions or judgments*. Include what you think is the *central idea* of this article with *relevant details* to support your position.

Part 2: What do you think the author wants her readers to learn about Marco Polo; what is the author's *purpose*? What do you think she was saying to readers about believing whether or not something is true *(fact)* when it isn't part of your own life experience; what is her *point of view*? How does she *convey that point of view*? Use one or more of the stories in the article to support your answer. **(Levels 2, 4, 5, 6)**

Creating a Scoring Guide for
Extended Answer Constructed-Response Questions

BOOK FOUR EXHIBIT 1.7

Constructed-Response
Extended Answer Scoring Guide

Advanced or Exemplary
- [ ] All "Goal" criteria *plus*:
- [ ] Supports author's point of view with more than one story or example
- [ ] Makes connection to similar point of view from a *different* story or article
- [ ] ncludes personal experience of similar situation

Goal
- [ ] Summarizes article without personal opinions or judgments
- [ ] Identifies central idea
- [ ] Provides relevant details to support central idea
- [ ] Identifies author's purpose
- [ ] Identifies author's point of view
- [ ] Explains how author conveys her point of view
- [ ] Supports identified point of view with one story or example from article

Progressing
- [ ] Meets four to six of the "Goal" criteria

Beginning
- [ ] Meets fewer than four of the "Goal" criteria
- [ ] Task to be repeated after reteaching
- [ ] Comments:

concepts, skills, and related Bloom's Taxonomy levels are represented in this one question. Student responses will provide powerful evidence as to the degree of their understanding of the targeted CCSS for this unit of study.

Step 10: Write Essential Question and Big Idea Directions

The final step of the CFA design process is to plan for students to respond to the unit's Essential Questions with the Big Ideas stated in their own words—either in writing or verbally. Whereas the selected-response and constructed-response questions are specif-

BOOK FOUR EXHIBIT 1.8

Generating Student Directions for Big Idea Responses to Essential Questions

Big Idea Responses to Essential Questions

Student Directions: Write a Big Idea response for each of the following Essential Questions. Include vocabulary terms you have learned. Your responses will be evaluated using the "Big Ideas Scoring Guide."

1. How can you convey a central idea when writing informative or expository texts?

2. What makes a summary of informational text effective?

3. How does an author of informational text convey a particular point of view or purpose?

ically based upon the "unwrapped" Priority Standards for the unit, students' verbal or written responses to the Essential Questions will provide evidence of what the students are likely to remember beyond the "borders" of that one unit of study. The simplest way to do this is to provide a third section on the CFA as shown in Exhibit 1.8, providing space for students to respond beneath each Essential Question. The same *generic* scoring guide (shown in Exhibit 1.9) can be used repeatedly on subsequent CFAs with different Essential Questions.

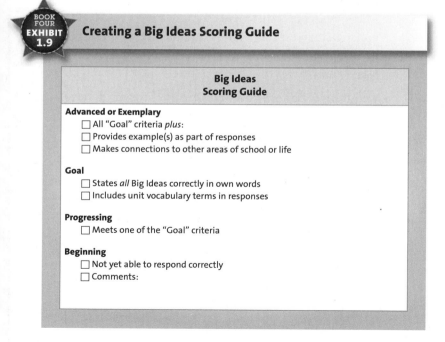

BOOK FOUR
EXHIBIT 1.9

Creating a Big Ideas Scoring Guide

**Big Ideas
Scoring Guide**

Advanced or Exemplary
- [ ] All "Goal" criteria *plus*:
- [ ] Provides example(s) as part of responses
- [ ] Makes connections to other areas of school or life

Goal
- [ ] States *all* Big Ideas correctly in own words
- [ ] Includes unit vocabulary terms in responses

Progressing
- [ ] Meets one of the "Goal" criteria

Beginning
- [ ] Not yet able to respond correctly
- [ ] Comments:

THE BENEFITS OF USING
COMMON FORMATIVE ASSESSMENTS

In Chapter Four, "Common Formative Assessments: The Center-piece of an Integrated Standards-Based Assessment System," presented in the assessment anthology *Ahead of the Curve* (Ainsworth, 2007, pp. 95–96), I highlighted several of the key benefits to educators who regularly use CFAs:

1. **Regular and timely feedback** regarding student attainment of most critical standards in order to better meet diverse learning needs of all students.

2. **Multiple-measure assessments** that allow students to demonstrate their understanding in a *variety of formats.* (This model of a three-part CFA: selected-response, constructed-response, and students' Big Idea responses to Essential Questions is an effective multiple-measure assessment.)

3. **Ongoing collaboration** opportunities for grade-level, course, and department teachers.

4. **Consistent expectations** within a grade level, course, and department regarding standards, instruction, and assessment priorities.

5. Agreed-upon **criteria for proficiency** to be met within each individual classroom, grade level, school, and district.

6. **Deliberate alignment** of classroom, school, district, and state assessments to better prepare students for success on high-stakes assessments.

7. **Predictive value** as to how students are likely to do on each succeeding assessment **in time to make instructional modifications.**

Educators who apply the process for creating a quality common formative assessment presented in this chapter will find they have a powerful tool for making highly accurate inferences regarding their students' understanding of the Common Core State Standards.

RECOMMENDATIONS FOR GETTING STARTED

Whenever I present the CFA process to educators and leaders throughout North America, I am often asked whether these formative assessments should be created by educators at the *school* level, or whether they can be created at the *district* level and then made available to educators for use in their own instructional programs. While I understand the reasons behind this request (the need to ensure consistency and quality across the system, the saving of time for busy educators, not adding one more thing to their plates, and so on), I always express my caution about leaving educators out of the assessment design process.

Understanding how a CFA is properly constructed, and why each of its components is necessary, is critical to educators knowing how to use it to maximum effect in the classroom. This must begin as a *teacher*-owned process—educators must first experience the design of a CFA *firsthand*. Only then does it make sense to think about ways to help educators "work smarter, not harder" in their use of common formative assessments on a regular basis.

One effective way to do this is to have educators initially experience the 10-step design process so they understand the thinking behind the various components of the CFA. Then, as they continue to create CFAs with grade-level or course-alike colleagues, ask them to share their CFAs with other educators in the school system by contributing to a secured district "bank" of CFAs, organized on the internal server by grade level, course, and content area. As educators use their CFAs in their own classrooms, they will want to edit and revise them. Because they understand how these assessment questions were initially created, they have the background understanding necessary to improve them. In addition, if everyone regards these assessments as "works in progress," educators will not be as reluctant to post them for all to see. They know they can at any time improve them as needed.

RESOURCES

Here is a list of very helpful resources to support the work of educators and leaders in creating and implementing quality common formative assessments:

- The Leadership and Learning Center's two-day seminar Common Formative Assessments (updated with a second edition seminar manual in 2011)

- *Common Formative Assessments: How to Connect Standards-Based Instruction and Assessment,* Ainsworth, L., and Viegut, D. (2006)

- *Ahead of the Curve: The Power of Assessment to Transform Teaching and Learning,* multiple authors, edited by Douglas B. Reeves. (2007)

- *Test Better, Teach Better: The Instructional Role of Assessment,* Popham, W. J. (2003)
- *Transformative Assessment,* Popham, W. J. (2008)
- *Standards, Assessment, & Accountability: Real Questions from Educators,* Reeves, D. B. (2010)
- *"Unwrapping" the Standards: A Simple Process to Make Standards Manageable,* Ainsworth, L. (2003)
- *Rigorous Curriculum Design: How to Create Curricular Units of Study that Align Standards, Instruction, and Assessment,* Ainsworth, L. (2010)

SUMMARY

The most effective assessments give an accurate picture of what students currently know and can do, so that educators can use the results to diagnose student learning needs and modify subsequent instruction accordingly. Presented here in summary form, the following 10 steps will help educators create effective assessments:

Step 1: Choose a focus for the unit of study

Step 2: Identify matching priority CCSS

Step 3: "Unwrap" the priority CCSS

Step 4: Create a graphic organizer

Step 5: Determine the Big Ideas

Step 6: Write the Essential Questions

Step 7: Write selected-response items

Step 8: Write constructed-response items (short and/or extended)

Step 9: Create scoring guides for constructed-response items

Step 10: Write Essential Question and Big Idea directions

Learning and applying the practical strategies presented in this chapter will do much to assist educators in "getting to know" the Common Core State Standards and in designing appropriate assessments to determine their students' understanding of them. CFAs—based on the "unwrapped" concepts, skills, and levels of rigor for a unit of study—will provide educators with the valuable diagnostic data they need in order to monitor and adjust instruction to meet the individualized learning needs of each student. As a result, students will have a much better chance of experiencing success on assessments aligned to the Common Core in English language arts and math *and* on assessments aligned to the state standards in all other content areas.

Whenever implementing new professional practices, the message must continually be: start small, build slowly. When educators first create a CFA for one unit of study, and then begin to implement the components in their own instructional programs (identifying specific Priority Standards; "unwrapping" those standards to pinpoint the teachable concepts, skills, and levels of rigor; using Big Ideas and Essential Questions; and applying the guidelines for writing effective assessment questions and scoring guides), they need time to experiment and become familiar with all of these new elements. But as their familiarity and comfort level with this standards-based assessment design process increases, so will the *frequency* of their use of CFAs. Remind everyone as often as needed, "It's a *process*, not an event."

References

Ainsworth, L. (2003). *"Unwrapping" the standards: A simple process to make standards manageable.* Englewood, CO: Lead + Learn Press.

Ainsworth, L. (2007). Common formative assessments: The centerpiece of an integrated standards-based assessment system. In *Ahead of the curve: The power of assessment to transform teaching and learning.* Bloomington, IN: Solution Tree.

Ainsworth, L. (2010). *Rigorous curriculum design: How to create curricular units of study that align standards, instruction, and assessment.* Englewood, CO: Lead + Learn Press.

Ainsworth, L., & Viegut, D. (2006). *Common formative assessments: How to connect standards-based instruction and assessment.* Thousand Oaks, CA: Corwin.

Anderson, L., & Krathwohl, D. A. (2001). *Taxonomy for learning, teaching and assessing: A revision of Bloom's taxonomy of educational objectives.* New York: Longman.

Common Core State Standards Initiative (CCSSI). (2010a). *Common Core State Standards for English language arts & literacy in history/social studies, science, and technical subjects* (PDF document). Retrieved from www.corestandards.org/assets/CCSSI_ELA%20Standards.pdf

Common Core State Standards Initiative (CCSSI). (2010b). Webinar. Retrieved Jan. 4, 2012, from www.schools.utah.gov/sars/DOCS/resources/ccsjune10webinar.aspx

Leadership and Learning Center, The. *Common formative assessments* (seminar). www.leadandlearn.com

Popham, W. J. (2003). *Test better, teach better: The instructional role of assessment.* Alexandria, VA: ASCD.

Popham, W. J. (2008). *Transformative assessment.* Alexandria, VA: ASCD.

Reeves, D. B. (ed.). (2007). *Ahead of the curve: The power of assessment to transform teaching and learning.* Bloomington, IN: Solution Tree.

Reeves, D. B. (2010). *Standards, assessment, & accountability: Real questions from educators with real answers from Douglas B. Reeves.* Englewood, CO: Lead + Learn Press.

Webb, L. N. (1997). Criteria for alignment of expectations and assessments in mathematics and science education. Research monograph no. 8. Council of Chief State School Officers. (Guide to Webb's Depth of Knowledge levels retrieved from www.aps.edu/rda/documents/resources/Webbs_DOK_Guide.pdf).

Wiliam, D. (2008). Changing classroom practice. *Educational Leadership, 65*(4), 36–41.

Mapping Out the Learning Journey: "Unwrapping" the Common Core State Standards

Lisa Almeida

Would you jump in the car to travel to an unknown destination without visiting Google Maps or punching the address into a navigational system? Would you embark on a trip to a foreign country without an itinerary? Educators are notorious for wanting to do everything right (and understandably so). To ensure a successful journey of learning, "unwrapping" the standards is a critical initial step for any practitioner using any new academic standards. Larry Ainsworth (2010, p. 35) says, "'Unwrapping' the standards means *analyzing* and *deconstructing* grade-level and course-specific standards for a unit of study to determine exactly what students need to know (concepts) and be able to do (skills)." Regardless of the teacher's years of experience, "unwrapping" is essential to truly dissecting the students'—and ultimately the teacher's—learning outcomes or end destination.

WHY DO YOU NEED TO "UNWRAP" THE STANDARDS?

"Unwrapping" the standards is a process that illuminates exactly what students are responsible for learning and what teachers are responsible for teaching. The process engages practitioners in focused, higher-level thinking and dialogue with each other. The process is contagious because of the powerful, hands-on professional development that ignites the initial excitement of the planning, teaching, and learning that is to come.

Many educators have shared with me that they had never had such standards-based, instructionally focused, and productive conversations with their colleagues until they experienced "unwrapping." Furthermore, some educators expressed that they were much more confident in speaking about standards and standards-based education to their peers, students, parents, leadership, and the community after they experienced "unwrapping."

Simply put, the "unwrapping" the standards process empowers educators to *know* and *conceptually understand* the desired end destination. Moreover, it equips educators to effectively and confidently communicate that desired end destination to all stakeholders. The process is a win-win situation for all involved.

WHAT DO YOU "UNWRAP" AND WHERE DO YOU START?

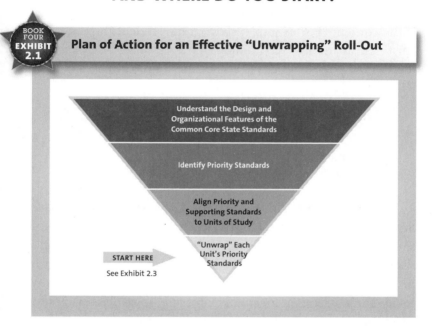

BOOK FOUR
EXHIBIT
2.1

Plan of Action for an Effective "Unwrapping" Roll-Out

Understand the Design and Organizational Features of the Common Core State Standards

Identify Priority Standards

Align Priority and Supporting Standards to Units of Study

"Unwrap" Each Unit's Priority Standards

START HERE
See Exhibit 2.3

HOW DO YOU START?

Everyone from leadership to teachers needs to experience "unwrapping." It is critical that practitioners know the higher-level thinking that is required during the process.

The process begins with "simply" identifying nouns and/or noun phrases (the content students need to know), and verbs (the skills; the application the students are required to perform with the knowledge). The next step asks educators to analyze (a level-four skill in the cognitive thinking process) the approximate level of rigor that will be required of students. The educators must analyze the skills in the context of the content. How complex is the content? For example, sixth-grade students are asked to "distinguish among fact, opinions, and reasoned judgment in a text" in the English language arts Common Core State Standard RH.6–8.8.

> (1)* IDENTIFY
> - (1) Facts
> - (1) Opinions
> - (3) Reasoned judgment

"Identify" is the skill that is at the lowest level of complexity. Sixth graders' ability to identify facts and opinions should be a simplistic task. However, identifying reasoned judgment requires students to conceptually understand reasoned judgment, which necessitates the ability to infer. Any educator knows the difficulty many students experience with inferring, regardless of grade. Therefore, the standard that appears to have a cognitive process level of one quickly increases to a minimum of a level three, in application.

In my experience in training and implementation support of "unwrapping" the standards, usually educators approach the work by either "unwrapping" the standards per unit of instruc-

---

*The number in parentheses represents the approximate level of cognitive process, as described in Bloom's Taxonomy (1956), Bloom's Revised Taxonomy (Anderson and Krathwohl, 2001), Marzano's New Taxonomy of Educational Objectives (Kendall and Marzano, 2007), or Webb's Depth of Knowledge (Webb, 1997).

tion or allocating "unwrapping" times, such as teacher work days, Saturdays, or common planning time. The latter option allows teams to "make a bigger dent" in the prioritized standards. Additionally, it cues them in to future essential instruction and learning, especially since the standards are new to everyone. As the unit approaches, teachers know the bulk of the foundation work is done. Many choose to review the Big Edeas and Essential Questions to make sure the foundational understanding and stimulating questions are the best they can be. Moreover, they share the "unwrapped" standard(s) with students, parents, supporting teachers, educational assistants, and leadership in preparation for the upcoming unit.

It is pivotal that teachers work in collaborative teams, or Data Teams, when completing the "unwrapping" process. The collective wisdom of the team ensures a more comprehensive understanding of learning objectives.

WHEN DO YOU START?

It is better to begin the "unwrapping" collaboration sooner rather than later. Leadership, district, school, grade-level, and/or course teams need to agree on a plan of action as soon as possible. Professional development may need to be planned for as soon as the current school year finishes. Therefore, teachers have the option of beginning the work during the summer. Many want to apply their learning immediately, so they can solidify the process. Others may choose to "unwrap" the first few units of instruction, so they are prepared for the first few weeks of school. Then they will "unwrap" as they plan for future instruction during common planning times or prior to a new Data Teams cycle.

If educators choose the latter option, I highly recommend scheduling the preplanning work—the "unwrapping"—many weeks in advance of the actual instruction. Remember that the process will shed light on the specific *concepts* (the knowledge the students will gain) and *skills* (the application) that students will be expected to master and teachers will be expected to effectively teach. For that reason, teachers need to build in ample time to prepare for the instruction.

Educators may need to familiarize themselves with specific content or even engage in professional development specific to the content, since the Common Core State Standards are more rigorous at each grade level than previous state standards. There is a good chance the new expectations may be completely new to a teacher's repertoire. It is critical that teachers work in collaborative teams, not in isolation, as they "unwrap" the standards. Moreover, it is essential that whoever is involved with instruction and/or is responsible for student achievement experience the "unwrapping" process. Everyone needs to know and be familiar with the end destination—the learning goals.

WHAT ARE THE NEXT STEPS AFTER "UNWRAPPING"?

After a unit is "unwrapped" and, therefore, the instructional and learning journeys are clear, teams should create the corresponding pre- and post-CFAS (common formative assessments). Now that there is a clear beginning and end to the destination, think of the pre- and post-assessments as bookends. The lesson plans are the books that will teach the identified concepts and skills.

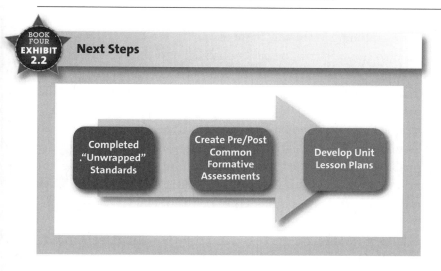

Because the Common Core State Standards are new, it is highly recommended that the team revisit these critical three steps after the instructional window closes (Exhibit 2.2). It is a good idea to make necessary changes to the foundation, the "unwrapped" standard(s), the assessments, and/or the unit plans as soon as possible. The team should schedule time in their collaborative planning that will be dedicated to "closing out" the particular unit. In that way, the practice of revising becomes part of the normal routine of instructional planning.

WHAT DOES "UNWRAPPING" LOOK LIKE?

The teacher team has gathered, has the necessary materials, such as standards and technology, and is ready to begin the work of "unwrapping." More and more teams choose to work electronically, so the work can be easily changed and shared with others. The process is contagious; many educators, including myself, continue to "unwrap" *everything*. For example, teachers use the process to "unwrap" text and definitions with students. I "unwrap" numerous standards, job descriptions, agendas, and to-do lists. I quickly learned that deconstructing, or "unwrapping," my husband's "honey-do" list was much more proactive, and got more accurate results. Moreover, an "unwrapped" to-do list is more efficient than a simple "laundry list" of items; it clearly communicates expectations.

Practitioners complete the steps shown in Exhibit 2.3 to successfully "unwrap" the standards.

BOOK
FOUR
EXHIBIT
2.3

Steps for "Unwrapping" Standards

Step	Directions
1: Identify key concepts and skills in unit's Priority Standard(s)	Underline key nouns and/or noun phrases that represent essential knowledge or concepts students will need to conceptually understand by the end of the unit. Don't worry if you underline "too much." That immediately illustrates that the standard contains a great deal of concepts/knowledge with perhaps minimal application.
	Next, identify the verbs, or the application that students are expected to "do" with the knowledge. Typically, the skills are circled, capitalized, or highlighted, so the application of the learning stands out amongst all the knowledge/concepts.
	Remember not to get into "grammatical wars" on whether or not a given word or phrase is a verb, is not a verb, is a prepositional phrase, etc. Simply ask the team, "What do students need to *know* about? What do the students need to *do* with that knowledge?" Those words need to be identified in step 1.
2: Create a graphic organizer	The team decides what nonlinguistic representation works best for their learning styles. Additionally, some teachers consider what format they can share with students and parents. For example, a first-grade team chose to illustrate their "unwrapped" standard in a tree. They placed the concepts/knowledge in the trunk and the skills/application on the branches. More common representations are a T-chart, semantic map, outline, and/or bulleted organizer.
	It is imperative that wording remain aligned to the Common Core State Standards document. For that reason, "rewording" of concepts and/or skills is not allowed. Educators are accountable to the CCSS document, not others' interpretation of the document.
3: Determine approximate level of rigor for each skill	After the skills are organized with the corresponding concepts, the team determines the *approximate* level of rigor. It is important to consider the skill *with* the concepts, not just the isolated skill. Place the number in parentheses next to the verb. It represents the approximate level of cognitive process as described in Bloom's Taxonomy, Bloom's Revised Taxonomy, Marzano's Taxonomy, or Webb's Depth of Knowledge.
	Make sure the purpose of the cognitive process number is communicated to all stakeholders (i.e., those who do not know the process).
4: Generate Big Ideas	Focus primarily on the concepts when generating Big Ideas. Two to four Big Ideas are recommended, since these are enduring knowledge students should retain for a lifetime. The Big Ideas are statements, complete sentences that students will be expected to communicate back to the teacher throughout or by the end of the unit. The concepts are concrete. The Big Ideas are demonstrations of the students' abstract thinking as they make connections with concepts and skills.
	Creating Big Ideas as adults requires higher-level thinking. The team is applying their understanding, analyzing and synthesizing as they generate the Big Ideas. Allow yourselves to be learners. Big Ideas may be adjusted as Essential Questions are created and/or after the completion of the unit. This is perfectly okay, and is, in fact, recommended. "Unwrapping" is a skill; it becomes easier and more efficient and achieves better results with more practice.
5: Create Essential Questions	Big Ideas are the *students' responses* to the Essential Questions. The Leadership and Learning Center recommends completing the Big Ideas first, so there is a clear end destination, which tends to be more difficult than generating questions. Typically, there are two to four Essential Questions. Teams need to make sure all Big Ideas have a corresponding Essential Question that will invite students into the learning process. However, there does not need to be one-to-one correspondence between Big Ideas and Essential Questions.
	Essential Questions are not typical questions students are asked. Think of engagement and real life when creating Essential Questions. What will excite the students in the upcoming learning? What wording will make them want to find and work towards the response—the Big Idea?
6. Check work with an "unwrapped" scoring guide	It is recommended that someone from outside the team who thoroughly understands and has applied the "unwrapping" process, such as a school or district Center-certified trainer, provide immediate feedback about steps 1–5. Steps 1–5, the foundation, need to be solid before instruction and assessments are planned.

Relationship of Concepts, Essential Questions, and Big Ideas

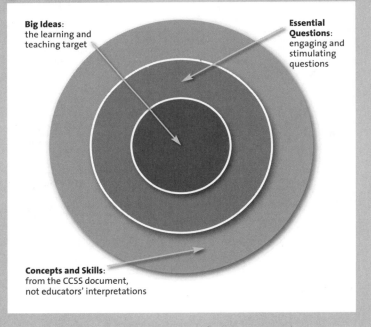

Big Ideas:
the learning and
teaching target

**Essential
Questions:**
engaging and
stimulating
questions

Concepts and Skills:
from the CCSS document,
not educators' interpretations

EXAMPLES OF "UNWRAPPED" STANDARDS

Example 1

Step 1: Identify key concepts and skills in unit's Priority Standard(s)

6.G.1: FIND the <u>area of right triangles, other triangles, special quadrilaterals, and polygons</u> by COMPOSING into <u>rectangles</u> or DECOMPOSING into <u>triangles and other shapes</u>; APPLY these <u>techniques</u> in the context of SOLVING <u>real-world</u> and <u>mathematical problems</u>.

Step 2: Create a graphic organizer

Concepts:
- Area
    - Right triangles
    - Other triangles
    - Special quadrilaterals
    - Polygons

- Rectangles
- Triangles
- Other shapes

- Techniques
    - Real-world problems
    - Mathematical problems

Skills:
    (2, 4) FIND
- Area
    - (2) Right triangles
    - (2) Other triangles
    - (4) Special quadrilaterals
    - (4) Polygons

    (6) COMPOSING
- Rectangles

    (6) DECOMPOSING
- Triangles
- Other shapes

    (3) APPLY
- Techniques

    (4, 5) SOLVING
- (5) Real-world problems
- (4) Mathematical problems

Step 3: Determine approximate level of rigor for each skill

Step 4: Generate Big Ideas

1. The area of a polygon can be determined by composing rectangles or by decomposing it into triangles.

2. Area is a measure of covering a two-dimensional shape expressed in square units. The area formula comes from the perpendicular relationship of base and height.

Step 5: Create Essential Questions

1. How do you find the area of a polygon?

2. What is area and how can you develop the area formula?

Example 2

Step 1: Identify key concepts and skills in unit's Priority Standard(s)

W.5.2: WRITE informative/explanatory texts to EXAMINE a topic and CONVEY ideas and information clearly.

Step 2: Create a graphic organizer

Concepts:

- Informative/explanatory texts
  - Topic
  - Ideas
  - Information

Skills:

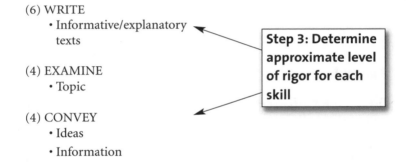

(6) WRITE
  - Informative/explanatory texts

(4) EXAMINE
  - Topic

(4) CONVEY
  - Ideas
  - Information

Step 3: Determine approximate level of rigor for each skill

Step 4: Generate Big Ideas
1. Informative/explanatory texts are used to analyze a topic.
2. It is imperative that a writer clearly communicates ideas and information.

Step 5: Create Essential Questions
1. Why would a writer choose to use informative/explanatory writing?
2. What does a writer need to remember when composing text?

BOOK FOUR
EXHIBIT 2.5

"Unwrapping" Template

Unit of Instruction:

Priority Standards:

Step	Notes	✔ If completed	✔ If there is a need to revisit at end of unit for possible revision
1: Identify key concepts and skills in unit's Priority Standard(s)			
2: Create a graphic organizer			
3: Determine approximate level of rigor for each skill			
4: Generate Big Ideas			
5: Create Essential Questions			
6. Check work with "unwrapping" scoring guide (Exhibit 2.6)			

BOOK FOUR EXHIBIT 2.6

"Unwrapping" Scoring Guide

	Proficient	Exemplary (All of proficient criteria, *plus*)	Comments
"Unwrapped" Priority Standard	• Include separate lists of *all* concepts (what students need to know) and skills (what students need to be able to do) on graphic organizer • Connect skills to concepts (with parenthetical or side-by-side notation) • Identify approximate cognition level (Bloom's, Webb, etc.) for each skill	• Add other higher-level skills if ones in Priority Standards are lower-level	
Big Ideas	• Represent explicit responses to Essential Questions • Are written succinctly and as complete statements (five to 10 words recommended) • Reflect essential connections students are to make and retain after instruction concludes • Convey value or long-term benefit of learning to students • Are written as *topical* statements (specific to particular content area focus) • Link directly to "unwrapped" standards, not to curriculum materials • Represent *all* "unwrapped" standards collectively	• Represent foundational understandings from which further generalizations can be derived • Are written in both teacher wording and student-friendly wording	
Essential Questions	• Lead students to discovery of Big Ideas on their own • Link directly to "unwrapped" standards and Big Ideas • Forecast learning goals for unit of study • Are written in student-friendly language • Reflect both lower and higher levels of questioning—"one-two punch" questions (e.g., knowledge and application) •Posted in classroom to focus instruction and assessment	• Are engaging (not routine questions) • Arouse student interest; require discussion, thought, investigation to answer • Link or extend to interdisciplinary connections	

Source: The Leadership and Learning Center, 2008.

For additional information on "unwrapping" the standards, Larry Ainsworth's *"Unwrapping" the Standards: A Simple Process to Make Standards Manageable* (2003) and Tracey Shiel's *Engaging Students Through Performance Assessments* (2010) are invaluable resources that expand on the process. More information is also available at www.leadandlearn.com.

LET'S GET STARTED

"Unwrapping" the standards is a process that makes the learning objectives manageable for teachers, support staff, leaders, parents, and students. Once the teaching and learning journey is clearly mapped out through "unwrapping," the destination becomes very evident to everyone. Additionally, once the "unwrapping" is done, it will be 90 percent complete. The only time it will need to be revisited is to make minor adjustments after implementation and/or when the Common Core State Standards are updated. Many educators have shared that this simple, yet powerful process changed their teaching and was one of the most powerful professional development and learning tools they have experienced. There has never been a better time to plan for strategic implementation of the Common Core State Standards. It starts with prioritization (not elimination) and "unwrapping" the standards.

SUMMARY

- Leadership needs to create and communicate a plan of action for an effective "unwrapping" roll-out. The plan should include, as a minimum, the following steps:

1. Understand the design and organizational features of the Common Core State Standards

2. Identify Priority Standards

3. Align Priority and supporting standards to units of study

4. "Unwrap" each unit's Priority Standards

- Logical next steps are to create pre- and post-CFAs and unit plans for each Priority Standard.

- Create a quality-control system that provides timely coaching and feedback to educators.

- Implement the necessary professional development and support structures to start the work as soon as possible.

References

Ainsworth, L. (2003). *"Unwrapping" the standards: A simple process to make standards manageable.* Englewood, CO: Lead + Learn Press.

Ainsworth, L. (2010). *Planning for rigorous curriculum design* (seminar handbook). Englewood, CO: Lead + Learn Press.

Anderson, L., & Krathwohl, D. A. (2001). *Taxonomy for learning, teaching and assessing: A revision of Bloom's taxonomy of educational objectives.* New York: Longman.

Bloom, B. S., et al. (1956). *Taxonomy of educational objectives: The classification of educational goals.* New York: Longmans, Green.

Common Core State Standards Initiative (CCSSI). (2010a). *Common Core State Standards for English language arts & literacy in history/social studies, science, and technical subjects* (PDF document). Retrieved from www.corestandards.org/assets/ CCSSI_ELA%20Standards.pdf

Common Core State Standards Initiative (CCSSI). (2010b). *Common Core State Standards for mathematics* (PDF document). Retrieved from www.corestandards.org/assets/CCSSI_Math %20Standards.pdf

Kendall, J., & Marzano, R. (2007). *The new taxonomy of educational objectives.* 2nd ed., Thousand Oaks, CA: Corwin.

Leadership and Learning Center, The. (2008). *Common formative assessments* (seminar manual). Englewood, CO: Lead + Learn Press.

Shiel, T. (2010). *Engaging students through performance assessments.* Englewood, CO: Lead + Learn Press.

Webb, L. N. (1997). Criteria for alignment of expectations and assessments in mathematics and science education. Research monograph no. 8. Council of Chief State School Officers. (Guide to Webb's Depth of Knowledge levels retrieved from www.aps.edu/ rda/documents/resources/Webbs_DOK_Guide.pdf).

THREE

Leveraging Data Teams and Professional Learning Communities for Success on the Common Core

Laura Besser

Data Teams are the single best way to help educators and administrators move from "drowning in data" to using information to make better instructional decisions. What makes the Data Teams process distinctive is that we are not just looking at student scores, but at the combination of student results, teaching strategies, and leadership support. The essential question is, "What can we do tomorrow to help students and teachers achieve their goals?" Data Teams give professionals respect, reinforcement, and feedback—the keys for improved impact on student learning.

—Douglas Reeves (2010)

The Common Core establishes a set of clear and consistent goals for learning that will ultimately prepare students for college and the workforce. Complete with specific learning pathways, the CCSS make the Data Teams process come alive because of the intentional alignment of standards between grade levels.

Data Teams see great gains in student learning because teachers are given the structure and time to collaboratively improve their instructional practice, which includes the use of standards and assessment in the classroom.

Data Teams are a model for professional collaboration, with the goal of improving instructional practice and thus improving learning for all students. Teachers on a Data Team share a common focus/standard, a common measurement tool (formative assessment), and a common way to evaluate student performance (scoring guide/answer key). Therefore, teams use a data-driven process and walk away at the end of a 60-minute meeting with a plan to accelerate student learning by providing targeted, researched-based, explicit instructional interventions. Teams function in a continuous improvement cycle, as they will continue to use the process every one to two weeks.

Instructional Data Teams marry two powerful practices: data and collaboration (McNulty and Besser, 2011). Effective teams use data and they use it in an ongoing way. When the Data Teams process is used effectively, teams establish goals, have discussions about instructional practice, monitor implementation and effectiveness, evaluate impact of strategies on student learning, provide feedback on use of strategies, and monitor the effectiveness of the process.

Just as Data Teams are a vehicle for professional conversations, Professional Learning Communities (PLCs) are also a means for teachers to have conversations around instruction and student learning. DuFour and Eaker (1998) have asserted that the strongest way to improve student learning is to help teachers function as PLCs. The authors describe characteristics of effective PLCs:

1. Shared mission, vision, values

2. Collective inquiry

3. Collaborative teams

4. Action-orientated and experimental

5. Continuous improvement

6. Results-orientated

The work of Data Teams and PLCs are driven by the same student-centered questions:

1. What is it we want students to learn?

2. How will we know if students are learning?

3. How will we respond when some of our students are not learning?

4. How will we enrich and extend learning for those students that are already proficient?

These questions are addressed in this chapter through the lens of a Data Team, including the connection to CCSS. This volume of the *Getting Ready for the Common Core Handbook Series* is focused on assessment, but it's difficult to separate the concepts and practices of standards, assessment, and instruction—in fact, it's ineffective to do so. All of these practices are embedded in the Data Teams process.

The Data Teams flow chart in Exhibit 3.1 illustrates the recommended process teams use to structure their model and approach to improve instruction. Each step will be described in detail, with connections to the CCSS, on the following pages.

BOOK FOUR EXHIBIT 3.1

The Data Teams Flow Chart

1. Examine the expectations. Look at the state standards or frameworks, district power standards, "unwrapped" standards.

10. Return to step 1. Begin the process again with the next critical expectation based on the pacing guide.

2. Develop a curriculum map. Create a year-long pacing chart/calendar.

3. Develop a common post-assessment. What must students master as a result of your teaching?

9. Meet as a team to determine if the goal was met. Determine next steps for students who did not reach proficiency on the assessment.

4. Administer the common formative assessment (pre-instruction). You need to know where students are in their learning before instruction occurs. What data tell you that the lessons you are preparing are the lessons students need?

8. Score the assessent and submit the data to the Data Team leader.

5. Follow the Data Teams Process for Results.
1—Collect and chart data
2—Analyze data and practice needs
3—Set, review, and revise incremental SMART goals
4—Select common instructional strategies
5—Determine results indicators
6—Monitor and evaluate results

7. Administer the common formative assessment (post-instruction).

6. Teach students using common instructional strategies.

1. STANDARDS IN THE DATA TEAMS PROCESS

In previous chapters, you've read about the CCSS and the expected impact of the standards on student learning. These rigorous learning expectations have the potential to transform education—teaching, learning, and leadership. What is it we want kids to learn? We want students to learn concepts and skills that are essential for life in the 21st century. We want kids to develop understandings and skills that will equip them for success in postsecondary education, in the workplace, and in life.

Teams begin the process by building a foundation. As you can see from the flow chart (Exhibit 3.1), the groundwork begins with the critical examination of academic standards.

Impact of Prioritizing Standards in the Data Teams Process

Data Teams use Priority Standards in their quest to improve teaching and learning. Schools and districts often take the first steps of prioritizing standards using a very specific set of criteria: what do students need to know and be able to do to be successful in school, life, and high-stakes assessments? The prioritizing process helps educators by investing greater amounts of time and resources on the standards that matter most for student success. This prioritized set of standards will often be used as a curriculum map or pacing guide. Data Teams then will further prioritize the most essential standards by using assessment data of students in their classrooms. Data Teams are driven by the purpose and desire to help every student reach high levels of proficiency with the most essential standards. In other words, "all means all"—every student is expected to reach proficiency in the standard that is taught in a Data Teams cycle.

> **CCSS Connection:** While the CCSS represent learning expectations that are rigorous, specific, and much clearer, there are still far too many standards (Ainsworth, 2010; Reeves, 2011). Data Teams must use the prioritized CCSS to drive their academic focus, as these standards have been determined to have the greatest impact on student success.

Impact of "Unwrapping" the Standards in the Data Teams Process

The "unwrapping" process is critical for Data Team success, because it is through this process that teams can translate standards into explicit success criteria, formative assessments, and micro learning experiences. Data Teams also teach, monitor, and assess small "chunks" of learning, and these mini foci are determined by peeling a standard and identifying all of the concepts and skills embedded within the statement.

Through the "unwrapping" process, teams can get a much better sense of what success looks like when students are taking control of the skill/concept and working towards mastery. After "unwrapping," teams develop success criteria that help guide their instruction, help provide feedback to students, and involve students in the Data Teams process through goal-setting and self-reflection on ongoing performance.

It is also critical that teams closely examine this standard prior to creating or finding a Data Teams assessment. When teams "unwrap" a standard prior to creating or selecting an assessment, they have better alignment to the cognitive demand and context of the standards.

Teams will eventually create learning experiences that will give students practice and opportunity to take control of the "unwrapped" concepts and skills.

> **CCSS Connection:** The rigor and clarity embedded in the CCSS help guide Data Teams when creating success criteria, formative assessment, and learning opportunities for students. When teams "unwrap" the CCSS, they will develop a common, clear understanding of the standards. Therefore, it is critical that all members are involved in the process (Reeves, 2002). The "unwrapping" process of the CCSS will also help teams develop better understandings of the "spiraling" nature of the standards, which will help teams when they are designing success criteria for the unit of instruction.

2. CREATING A DATA TEAMS ROAD MAP

Data Teams create road maps to guide their team focus throughout the year. The road map is comprised of Priority Standards—and may even be prioritized again by examining data specific to the student population and representing their most urgent needs. The road map is not used as a pacing guide (content covered in day-to-day classroom instruction); it serves as a planning tool, but can be revised based on formative data. Data Teams do not "abandon" an area of focus (Priority Standard) until their students have reached the desired level of proficiency. All students are expected to reach proficiency, and Data Teams will continue to provide intervention, time, and resources until all students are successful in the most essential standards.

> **CCSS Connection:** The CCSS represent the most essential standards for student success, therefore should be used when creating a road map. Data Teams will examine the standards as well as the formative data of their students when determining the most logical progression for their students.

3 AND 4. ASSESSMENT IN THE DATA TEAMS PROCESS

Standards and assessment are foundational blocks in the Data Teams process. Standards provide the drive—or the "what"—behind the team focus, and the assessment is the means to collect data on student learning and use it to inform instruction.

Through the research of Marzano (2010) and Hattie (2009) we have learned about the powerful impact of both frequent and formative assessments. Data Team assessments are short-cycle interim assessments that measure a small "chunk" of learning (identified from the "unwrapped" standard). The assessment is used to gather real-time data on the impact and effectiveness of instruction. The assessment will also provide evidence as to the current state of proficiency in relation to the learning goal.

One of the biggest mistakes teams make is getting stuck in the "pre-/post-assessment" mentality where they are using formative assessments, but in a summative manner. Data Teams embrace assessment as a cycle, a cycle that is formative in nature and that continues until student goals are reached. Data Teams embrace assessment for learning (measuring learning as it is occuring, not after it has occured).

> **CCSS Connection:** The rigor of the CCSS demands a more robust assessment, and many of the current or traditional assessments will not be sufficient as measurement tools. Data Teams will need to deliberately and explicitly create (or select) assessments that will provide information that is accurate and valid and will measure the specificity and rigor outlined in the CCSS.

5. THE DATA TEAMS STEP-BY-STEP MEETING PROCESS

The essence of data-driven decision making is not about perfection and finding the decision that is popular, it's about finding the decision that is most likely to improve student achievement, produce the best results for the most students, and promote the long term goals of equity and excellence.

—Douglas Reeves (2002)

This data-driven process is used in every Data Team meeting (60–90 minutes). Exhibit 3.2 illustrates the five-step meeting

The Data Teams Process for Results

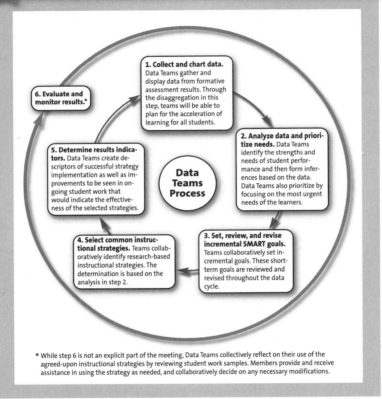

1. Collect and chart data. Data Teams gather and display data from formative assessment results. Through the disaggregation in this step, teams will be able to plan for the acceleration of learning for all students.

6. Evaluate and monitor results.*

5. Determine results indicators. Data Teams create descriptors of successful strategy implementation as well as improvements to be seen in ongoing student work that would indicate the effectiveness of the selected strategies.

Data Teams Process

2. Analyze data and prioritize needs. Data Teams identify the strengths and needs of student performance and then form inferences based on the data. Data Teams also prioritize by focusing on the most urgent needs of the learners.

4. Select common instructional strategies. Teams collaboratively identify research-based instructional strategies. The determination is based on the analysis in step 2.

3. Set, review, and revise incremental SMART goals. Teams collaboratively set incremental goals. These short-term goals are reviewed and revised throughout the data cycle.

* While step 6 is not an explicit part of the meeting, Data Teams collectively reflect on their use of the agreed-upon instructional strategies by reviewing student work samples. Members provide and receive assistance in using the strategy as needed, and collaboratively decide on any necessary modifications.

process. The process is structured so that conversation can focus on students and learning, and teachers and instruction.

Step 1: Collect and Chart the Data

Teams disaggregate information on student learning using data from a short-cycle common formative assessment. The visual display of data (Exhibit 3.3) allows teachers to have targeted conversations about students and their proficiency levels. Teachers usually complete this step prior to the 60-minute meeting and come prepared to talk about individual student and classroom results.

> **CCSS Connection:** The nature of the spiraling effect and specific learning progressions in the CCSS can drive the organization of the assess-

BOOK FOUR
EXHIBIT 3.3

Data Teams Chart Template

Teacher	Names/ Number of students with advanced proficiency	Names/ Number of proficient students	Names/ Number of students close to proficiency	Names/ Number of students below proficiency	Names/ Number of students far below proficiency
Total					

ment data. Teams can elect to disaggregate by proficiency levels as well as objectives in the CCSS.

Step 2: Analyze Student Performance Data and Prioritize Needs

Teams first gain insight by carefully examining student performance and learning levels. The teams analyze student assessments to identify trends and patterns both from performance on the

---

BOOK FOUR EXHIBIT 3.4

Data Teams Analysis Template

Student Performance Behaviors	Inferences
Advanced Proficiency Strengths: Next Steps:	
Proficient Strengths: Next Steps:	
Close to Proficiency Strengths: Obstacles:	
Below Proficiency Strengths: Obstacles:	
Far Below Proficiency Strengths: Obstacles:	

common formative assessment and then with the success criteria as described on the scoring guide or answer key as they are used when determining student proficiency levels. Teams conduct a deeper level of analysis by forming evidence-based conclusions about learning. Teams perform a root cause analysis and will have a dialogue that begins with the "what"—identification of strengths and needs based on the scoring guide or answer key; to the "why"—cognitive factors that are either contributing to student success or are acting as a barrier to their learning. Ideally, this depth of root cause analysis is conducted for every proficiency level represented in step 1.

> **CCSS Connection:** The specificity (from the "unwrapped" standard) and rigor embedded in the CCSS will drive the conversation in this step of the process. While the first part of the conversation is focused on performance on the assessment, the second part of the team dialogue should reflect the deep rigorous performance required of students by this standard as well as the learning progressions in relation to the rigor of standards, teaching, and learning.

Step 3: Set, Review, and Revise Incremental SMART Goals

Teams set incremental goals for student learning. It is easy for teams to write SMART goals (specific, measurable, attainable, relevant, and timely), but it is more difficult to use them to analyze, monitor, and adjust professional practice. The obvious target is for all students to reach proficiency or advanced proficiency, but since the goals are incremental—monitored on a frequent basis (every 2–3 weeks)—they are results-driven. While all students may not reach proficiency in the first cycle, teams should see acceleration from one proficiency level to the next. Goals are then reviewed at the next meeting and revised to reflect new baseline data.

> **CCSS Connection:** The specificity of the CCSS supports the approach to crafting SMART goals. The learning goals are specific and measurable. They also represent the relevant and necessary concepts and skills students need to be successful in school and in life.

BOOK FOUR EXHIBIT 3.5

SMART Goal Template

Percentage of _____ scoring at proficiency or higher in _____ will

increase from _____ to _____ by _____ as measured by _____

administered on _____.

Step 4: Select Instructional Strategies

Data Teams see the immediate results of their instruction when they use a very formal and explicit approach to collaboratively planning data-driven interventions:

1. Revisit step 2 in the Data Teams process—the root cause of student learning.

2. Brainstorm research-based strategies that will most likely impact the root cause of learning.

3. Deliberately select one to two strategies that are most likely to impact student achievement (as measured on an assessment) and student learning (the root cause).

4. Develop shared understandings of the strategies and commit to using the strategies with fidelity. Ideally, this same deliberate and explicit process is repeated for every level of proficiency.

CCSS Connection: The CCSS will be a failed initiative if we do not improve the quality of instruction in the classroom. Step 4 of the Data Teams

BOOK FOUR
EXHIBIT
3.6

Instructional Strategies Template

Step 2—Analysis of Student Learning (root causes/inferences)	Step 4—Instructional Strategies
Advanced Proficiency	
Proficient	
Close to Proficiency	
Below Proficiency	
Far Below Proficiency	

process provides educators the time and structure for the collaborative dialogue that will result in the improved instructional practice of teachers.

Step 5: Determine Results Indicators

Results indicators are statements that illustrate the implementation of strategies and impact of instruction on student learning. Teams paint the picture of what teaching and learning looks like in the classroom. Teachers implement strategies and monitor to see if their actions are having the desired impact on student learning. Teachers are self-monitoring the impact of strategies determined in the meeting, and all of the teachers have the same visual of what effective use of the strategy looks like. The development and use of results indicators allow teachers to monitor their ef-

BOOK
FOUR
EXHIBIT
3.7

Results Indicators Template

Step 4—Instructional Strategies	Step 5—Results Indicators "If we use (strategy) to impact (inference identified in step 2) then we will see (impact and effectiveness)"
Advanced Proficiency	
Proficient	
Close to Proficiency	
Below Proficiency	
Far Below Proficiency	

fectiveness and impact on student learning. Like SMART goals, these statements are very easy to write, but more difficult to use. Teams formally use results indicators in their monitoring meeting (step 6 of the Data Teams process) as a guide for their conversation. Like steps 2 and 4, if teams have analysis that reflects varied proficiency levels, and they have strategies specifically selected for those proficiency levels, they also need results indicator statements for each strategy.

> **CCSS Connection:** The Common Core paints a very clear picture of what learning looks like in the classroom. The learning progressions help teachers monitor individual growth of students. This step allows teachers to monitor the rigor of their instruction as high levels of teaching are neccessary in order for students to develop depth of knowledge as required in the CCSS. This step also provides tools for teachers to monitor their impact on student learning.

Step 6: Monitor and Evaluate Student Results

Data Teams engage in a formative process: teams are continuously monitoring and evaluating teaching and learning. When teachers return to their classrooms to use the agreed-upon strategies, they are immediately monitoring the quality of instruction as well as the immediate impact on learning. This step occurs outside of the traditional 60-minute Data Team meeting. While monitoring occurs in an "informal" meeting that is typically no longer than 30 minutes, teachers do have formal conversations. Teams use the results indicators and formative data to drive their conversations. Teachers share observations, perhaps some student work or anecdotal notes. They engage in collaborative dialogue on the effectiveness and impact of their implementation of the agreed-upon strategies. It is because they are having this formal conversation that they can celebrate short-term wins, and also make midcourse corrections by adjusting their use of the strategy or, in some cases, selecting another strategy if it is not having the desired impact on student learning.

> **CCSS Connection:** The design of the CCSS makes the learning progressions very clear, and therefore makes monitoring much more explicit as teachers can monitor the formative growth of students. Data Teams will monitor student progress towards the CCSS on a frequent basis and therefore teachers and students will be able to celebrate short-term results.

Exhibit 3.8 illustrates the Data Teams five-step meeting process (step 6 is conducted in a separate meeting held one to two weeks later) with a CCSS standard. The spiraling nature of the standard is easily interwoven into the process, and therefore allows for the learning progressions to be interwoven into the Data Teams process.

BOOK
FOUR
EXHIBIT
3.8

The Data Teams Process and the Common Core State Standards—Sample Minutes

Grade level: 5   **Date:** Jan. 10, 2012   **Subject:** Reading

Data Teams Steps 1 and 2

CCSS	#	%	Names	Strengths/Needs	Inferences
RI.6.1: Cite textual evidence to support analysis of what the text says explicitly as well as inferences drawn from the text.	2	10%	Ryan, Sara	Students read far above grade level.	Strong analysis skills from lots of practice reading higher-level books.
* RI.5.1: Quote accurately from a text when explaining what the text says explicitly and when drawing inferences from the text. (* on grade level)	8	40%	Mike, Blake, Ty, Brittany, Ciara, Emily, Jose, Maria	Students have good reading habits. They go back to the text for information and they reread when they become confused.	Students have learned the habits of good reading and know when to use them to enhance their comprehension.
Total proficient or above	10	50%			
RI.4.1: Refer to details and examples in a text when ex-plaining what the text says explicitly and when drawing inferences from the text.	3	15%	John, Lea, Denise	Students have good comprehension and reading habits. Students do not know how to identify quotes in a text.	Students know and remember details from the text due to good reading habits. They cannot distinguish details from quotes.
Total close to proficient	3	15%			
RI.3.1: Ask and answer questions to demonstrate understanding of a text, referring explicitly to the text as the basis for the answers.	4	20%	Mark, Brian, Marlon, Karen	Students can read with some assistance and comprehend enough to ask logical questions. Students struggle to read grade-level texts independently and lack critical reading skills.	Students have learned to read fluently and have basic comprehension skills. Students have not developed the habits of critical readers. They struggle to move beyond the literal level of text.
Total far to go	4	20%			
RI.2.1: Ask and answer such questions as *who, what, where, when, why,* and *how* to demonstrate understand-ing of key details in a text.	3	15%	Mario, Keisha, Shaun	Students demonstrate phonemic awareness. Students cannot comprehend grade-level texts due to poor reading and thinking skills. Language barriers affect one of the students.	Students have made some progress with intensive help in learning to read. Students struggle with texts that do not contain pictures and visual aids. They do not read fluently and struggle to compre-hend without assistance and guidance from the teacher. They do not read independently at home or for leisure.
Total intensive	3	15%			
Overall Total	20	100%			

BOOK FOUR EXHIBIT 3.8

The Data Teams Process and the Common Core State Standards—Sample Minutes *(continued)*

Data Teams Step 3

SMART Goal: The percentage of fifth graders scoring proficient or higher on CCSS RI.5.1: *Quote accurately from a text when explaining what the text says explicitly and when drawing inferences from the text*, will increase from 50% to 80% as measured by a formative assessment administered on January 24, 2012.

Data Teams Steps 4 and 5

CCSS	#	%	Research-Based Instructional Strategies	Results Indicators (Teachers)	Results Indicators (Students)
RI.6.1: Cite textual evidence to support analysis of what the text says explicitly as well as inferences drawn from the text.	2	10%	Create graphic organizers to help students move to the grade 8 standard in which they draw inferences as well as analyze the details that most strongly support an analysis of what the text says.	Teachers will provide an exemplar organizer as a model and then provide direct instruction to students to move their thinking to the grade 8 standard—being able to distinguish the details that *most strongly support* what the text says.	Students will be able to explain and justify their selections of details that strongly support their analysis of what the text says both orally and in written summary.
* RI.5.1: Quote accurately from a text when explaining what the text says explicitly and when drawing inferences from the text. (* on grade level)	8	40%	Use a similarities and differences graphic organizer to help students distinguish between quoting the text and citing evidence to support an analysis.	Teachers will provide an exemplar organizer that demonstrates the differences between quoting the text and citing evidence in the text to support an analysis. Teachers will provide direct instruction and practice activities to advance students to the grade 5 standard.	Students will accurately complete a similarities and differences organizer and explain their work in a written summary.
Total proficient or above	**10**	**50%**			
RI.4.1: Refer to details and examples in a text when explaining what the text says explicitly and when drawing inferences from the text.	3	15%	In small group, use direct instruction using quotes from the text and ask students to identify and analyze the quotes. They will discuss how the quotes represent what the text says and then practice pulling their own quotes based on scenarios given by the teacher.	Teachers will engage in modeling and oral metacognitive thinking to support students in their thinking. Students will be provided examples and practice activities to refine their skills.	Students will accurately complete practice activities quoting the text and explain their thinking in a written summary.
Total close to proficient	**3**	**15%**			
RI.3.1: Ask and answer questions to demonstrate understanding of a text, referring explicitly to the text as the basis for the answers.	4	20%	In small group, use direct instruction using details and examples from the text and engage in a think-aloud to show students how to pull relevant details from a text. Allow time for practice and move to quotes using the same process.	Teachers will engage in modeling and oral metacognitive thinking to support students in their thinking. Students will be provided examples and practice activities to refine their skills.	Students will accurately complete practice activities quoting the text and explain their thinking in a written summary.
Total far to go	**4**	**20%**			
RI.2.1: Ask and answer such questions as *who, what, where, when, why,* and *how* to demonstrate understanding of key details in a text.	3	15%	Include these students with the above group for small-group instruction as well as have the literacy teacher, ESL teacher, or special education teacher provide one-on-one instruction in a pull-out session, and/or accommodations as required.	Teachers will engage in modeling and oral metacognitive thinking to support students in their thinking. Students will be provided examples and practice activities to refine their skills. A focus on peer-to-peer speaking and use of visuals will be included.	Students will accurately identify quotes and details from the text and explain their thinking orally and in writing.
Total intensive	**3**	**15%**			

Source: Cathy Lassiter, The Leadership and Learning Center.

6. TEACHING STUDENTS USING COMMON INSTRUCTIONAL STRATEGIES

There is no deep secret called "teaching and learning": teaching and learning are visible in the classrooms of the successful teachers and students, teaching and learning are visible in the passion displayed by the teacher and learner when successful learning and teaching occurs, and teaching and learning require much skill and knowledge by both teacher and student.

—John Hattie (2009)

Learning is the ultimate goal of education, and the curriculum or standards provide the rigorous goals students are working towards. However, very few students will ever reach those rigorous goals without effective teachers. Hattie makes a seemingly obvious statement in *Visible Learning* (2009): "What teachers do matters." He then recounts it by saying that what "some" teachers do matters. The simple truth is that skilled teachers make a difference. Those who study the art and science of instruction and apply strategies in a systematic, deliberate, explicit manner see great gains in student learning. In his synthesis of over 800 meta-analyses, Hattie (2009) identified aspects of teaching approaches associated with student learning:

- Paying deliberate attention to learning instructions and success criteria
- Setting challenging tasks
- Providing multiple opportunities for deliberate practice
- Knowing when one (teacher and/or student) is successful in attaining these goals

- Understanding the critical role of teaching appropriate learning strategies
- Planning and talking about teaching
- Ensuring the teacher constantly seeks feedback information as to the success of his or her teaching for the students

These approaches have been proven to be effective and have dramatic impacts on learning. It would be difficult to become skilled at all of these approaches without having professional collaboration with colleagues. Hattie's approaches mesh perfectly with the Data Teams process. Every behavior listed above is embedded in the process.

CCSS Connection: How can the quality of instruction improve if teachers aren't given the time, opportunity, and structure to have collaborative conversations about teaching and learning? Schmoker (2005) calls isolation "the enemy of improvement." In other words, if we want teachers to implement the practices identified above, it most likely won't happen if teachers work in isolation. Isolation breeds ineffective practices and fails to tap the talent and strengths of the teachers in our schools. The rigorous nature of the CCSS will require teachers to collaborate around instruction. Teachers want to make a difference; let's give them the vehicle to have conversations around the most effective instructional practices and collaboratively create plans to deliver quality instruction.

7, 8, AND 9. ADMINISTER AND SCORE THE ASSESSMENT, AND SUBMIT SCORES TO THE DATA TEAM LEADER

These steps follow the teaching, learning, monitoring, and formative assessing that occurs in classrooms. Teams are formally measuring student learning through a common "post-" instruction assessment, described earlier. Teams often make the mistake of using this formative assessment as a summative measure; it's intended to measure the learning that is occurring in this teaching cycle. Students who don't meet the desired proficiency levels will have multiple opportunities in the next cycle to improve their understandings of the concepts and skills.

Data Teams work from a common standard, a common assessment, and a common scoring guide. The standard is the obvious learning goal, the assessment is a measurement tool, and the common scoring guide outlines learning behaviors. While teachers on a Data Team may score the assessments of students in their classes, in Douglas Reeves' groundbreaking "90/90/90" studies (2000) of schools with 90 percent of students eligible for free or reduced lunch, 90 percent of students belonging to ethnic minority groups, and 90 percent of students achieving proficiency in reading or another state or district standard, he identified "external scoring" as an effective practice. External scoring, also known as collaborative scoring, is a critical behavior in the Data Teams process, as teachers must reach agreement about the scoring to ensure consistency and common understanding (Ainsworth, 2010).

CCSS Connection: The learning progressions in the CCSS must obviously be measured and evaluated on a formative basis. It would be very difficult, if not impossible, to monitor, set formative goals, measure incremental learning, and identify immediate instructional interventions if teachers were not monitoring learning progressions on a formative basis. The Data Teams process provides the vehicle for the formative monitoring and evaluation that the CCSS require in order to measure student growth.

9 AND 10. CONTINUE THE PROCESS

If the goal is to make continuous improvement, then one of the primary responsibilities of the Data Teams must be to identify the needs of individuals and teams and provide the supports necessary for learning.

—McNulty and Besser (2011)

When looking at the Data Teams flow chart (Exhibit 3.1), you can see that step 9 is a time for teams to determine if they achieved the incremental learning goals. If teams reached the desired state of proficiency—for all students—then they will move their focus to the next academic standard outlined on the Data Teams road map. If they didn't reach their goal, then the teaching and learning process with the current academic standard will continue. The Data Teams cycle continues until the team reaches the desired state of proficiency.

USING THE COMMON CORE STATE STANDARDS TO GET RESULTS

If educators use the rigor and specificity outlined in the CCSS to guide assessment, instruction, and classroom learning, then high levels of teaching and learning happen in classrooms. This chapter highlighted the marriage of three practices: data, collaboration, and the CCSS. When each is used separately, you may see some results, but when the practices are effectively used together, amazing gains will happen in teaching, learning, and leadership.

The Leadership and Learning Center strongly believes that schools and districts across the country can use Data Teams as a high-leverage strategy to help deliver the hope and promise of the CCSS, and make educational transformation a reality.

SUMMARY

- Data Teams have two central purposes: to collaboratively improve student learning and to collaboratively improve the quality of instruction. Data Teams improve learning by keeping the focus on the academic growth of students and the achievement of learning goals. Data Teams improve the quality of instruction by providing research-based interventions to help accelerate the progress of all students.

- Standards and formative assessment are the foundational blocks of the Data Teams process. The CCSS provide teams with rigorous expectations for student success, and teams prioritize those standards by using data that illuminate the most urgent needs of their student population. Formative assessment in the Data Teams process helps teams to determine if students are making adequate progress towards the rigorous demands of the CCSS. The assessments in the Data Teams process also serve as a powerful method of feedback for students and teachers.

• Fidelity and effective use of the Data Teams process is imperative for student and team success. The process is designed so that teams use data well, and in a collaborative manner. When the process is used as a continuous improvement cycle, teams can systematically monitor teaching and learning.

• Monitoring is the key to effective growth in teaching and learning. When teams collaboratively monitor their instruction, they can make timely midcourse corrections. When teams collaboratively monitor student learning, they can provide the specific, timely, and accurate feedback students need in order to move to the next level of learning.

References

Ainsworth, L. (2010). *Rigorous curriculum design: How to create curricular units of study that align standards, instruction, and assessment.* Englewood, CO: Lead + Learn Press.

Anderson, K. (2010). *Data teams success stories, volume 1.* Englewood, CO: Lead + Learn Press.

Doubek, B. (2010). *Data teams: The big picture.* Englewood, CO: Lead + Learn Press.

DuFour, R., & Eaker, R. (1998). *Professional learning communities at work: Best practices for enhancing student achievement.* Bloomington, IN: Solution Tree.

Hattie, J. C. (2009). *Visible learning: A synthesis of over 800 meta-analyses relating to achievement.* New York: Routledge.

Leadership and Learning Center, The. (2010). *Data teams, 3rd edition* (seminar handbook). Englewood, CO: Lead + Learn Press.

Marzano, R. J. (2010). *Formative assessment and standards-based grading: Classroom strategies that work.* Bloomington, IN: Marzano Research Laboratory.

McNulty, B., & Besser, L. (2011). *Leaders make it happen: An administrator's guide to data teams.* Englewood, CO: Lead + Learn Press.

Popham, J. (2009). *Unlearned lessons: Six stumbling blocks to our schools' success.* Cambridge, MA: Harvard Education Press.

Reeves, D. B. (2000). *Accountability in action.* Englewood, CO: Advanced Learning Press.

Reeves, D. B. (2002). *A leader's guide to standards.* San Francisco, CA: Jossey-Bass.

Reeves, D. B. (2004). *Accountability for learning.* Alexandria, VA: ASCD.

Reeves, D. B. (2011, March). Getting ready for common standards. *American School Board Journal, 198*(3).

Schmoker, M. (2005). *Results now.* Alexandria, VA: ASCD.

Wiggs, M. (2011). *Standards and assessment: The core of quality instruction.* Englewood, CO: Lead + Learn Press.

Feedback and Formative Assessment to Advance Learning

Maryann D. Wiggs

Throughout this four-part *Getting Ready for the Common Core Handbook Series*, we have used the metaphor of the navigation system to define the terrain to be traveled in moving from awareness to implementation of the Common Core State Standards. The many authors in this series have provided detailed descriptions to increase educator understanding of the English language arts (ELA) and mathematics Common Core State Standards and provided specific "how-to" strategies for next steps on the implementation journey. A navigation system, by design, provides travelers with constant feedback regarding their current location in relation to the destination. Similarly, the Common Core State Standards have been written to be focused, clear, coherent, and specific, and can serve as the GPS device for both teachers and students to gain clear perspective on the location of any given learner on the road toward college, career, and citizenship readiness.

The design and organization of the Common Core State Standards provide a clear and detailed map of the concepts and skills students must master in each grade to be considered proficient. Thus, the resulting learning trajectories, or grade-level building blocks, can serve as guideposts along the route. When knowledge of the learning pathways is coupled with formative assessment practices, the result is a powerful force for advancing student achievement in meeting the rigorous expectations outlined in the Common Core State Standards. Effective feedback, then, is the fuel that advances student learning in the direction of the hope and the promise of the Common Core State Standards. This chapter on feedback and formative assessment to advance learning synthesizes information gleaned from the chapters on using common formative assessment, "unwrapping" the standards, and leveraging Professional Learning Communities and Data Teams as continuous improvement structures wherein feedback is central to supporting student attainment of the Common Core State Standards.

CONNECTING FEEDBACK AND COMMON FORMATIVE ASSESSMENT

Common formative assessment (CFA) is an ideal structure for gathering real-time information regarding the type of progress each individual student is making in demonstrating proficiency of the grade-specific Common Core State Standards (CCSS) embedded in a unit of study. Frequent use of common formative assessment results provides a context for connecting feedback on how well students are progressing toward demonstrating proficiency of the grade-specific CCSS. In fact, in Chapter One of this handbook, titled "Connecting Common Core State Standards with Common Formative Assessments," Larry Ainsworth advocates for using formative assessment results *diagnostically* to determine individual student needs and to inform instruction accordingly, during classroom instruction, the next day, or in the next unit of study. In his book *Ahead of the Curve* (2007),

Ainsworth notes one of the most important benefits of using common formative assessment results is that it enables educators to *diagnose* student learning needs accurately in time to make instructional modifications. In addition, common formative assessments provide students with timely feedback regarding their current level of understanding so that they can identify for themselves what they already know and what they have yet to learn. In these ways, both educators and students are able to utilize common formative assessment results to their maximum potential (Ainsworth, 2007, p. 96).

In short, common formative assessment is most beneficial to teachers and students when *both* use the results

1. as feedback to determine current level of proficiency; and

2. as feedback to *diagnose* future instructional adjustments.

Thus, it is this partnership between the teacher and the student acting upon the results of the common formative assessment, together, that creates the conditions for feedback, as a formative practice, to be intentionally used to advance student learning. In order for this partnership to be most effective, both teachers and students must have a clear understanding of the grade-specific standards that serve as the focuses (or goals) of the unit of study and the specific attributes of those goals that will be addressed in the common formative assessments embedded within. In addition, knowledge of how a given grade-specific standard fits into the larger CCSS learning progressions schema becomes extremely beneficial when diagnosing future instructional adjustments.

In their research on *The Power of Feedback*, John Hattie and Helen Timperley (2007) claim that the main purpose of feedback is to reduce discrepancies between current understandings and performance and the goal. Further, they go on to say that effective feedback must answer three major questions asked by a teacher and/or by a student:

- Where am I going? (What are the goals of learning?)
- How am I going? (What progress is being made toward the learning goal?)
- Where to next? (What activities need to be undertaken to make better progress?)

The learning progressions embedded in the Common Core State Standards provide an ideal context for connecting effective feedback in the arena of common formative assessment to specifically answer questions about where learning is going and the status of the learner at any given point, and provide an opportunity to clarify next steps along the learning pathway.

Exhibit 4.1 illustrates an ELA CCSS learning progression side-by-side with sample performance task items taken from Appendix B of the CCSS document. The far left column in the illustration provides the coding system for the reading for literature standard 2 from kindergarten to the college and career readiness (CCR) anchor standard. By tracing the learning progression in the middle column from **RL.K.2** to **RL.11–12.2** one can notice that the **R.CCR.2** anchor standard serves as the central point, or the significant learning expectation toward which all grade-specific standards aspire. As students move along the plane of a particular learning trajectory, they study the same expectation each year at ever-increasing levels of complexity and sophistication. The

BOOK FOUR EXHIBIT 4.1

CCSS Learning Progression Example

Illustration of an ELA CCSS Learning Progression and Related Sample Performance Tasks

Standard	ELA Common Core State Standards	Sample Performance Tasks
R.CCR.2	Determine central ideas or themes of a text and analyze their development; summarize the key supporting details and ideas.	*These brief sample performance tasks illustrate specifically the application of the standards to text with sufficient complexity, quality, and range.*
RL.11–12.2	Determine two or more themes or central ideas of a text and analyze their development over the course of the text, including how they interact and build on one another to produce a complex account; provide an objective summary of the text.	Students provide an *objective summary* of F. Scott Fitzgerald's *Great Gatsby* wherein they analyze how *over the course of the text* different characters try to escape the worlds they come from, including whose help they get and whether anybody succeeds in escaping.
RL.9–10.2	Determine a theme or central idea of a text and analyze in detail its development over the course of the text, including how it emerges and is shaped and refined by specific details; provide an objective summary of the text.	Students *analyze in detail* the theme of relationships between mothers and daughters and how that *theme develops over the course of* Amy Tan's *Joy Luck Club*. Students search the text for *specific details* that show how *the theme emerges and how it is shaped and refined* over the course of the novel.
RL.8.2	Determine a theme or central idea of a text and analyze its development over the course of the text, including its relationship to the characters, setting, and plot; provide an objective summary of the text.	Students *summarize the development* of the morality of Tom Sawyer in Mark Twain's novel of the same name and analyze its connection to themes of accountability and authenticity by noting how it is *conveyed through characters, setting, and plot.*
RL.7.2	Determine a theme or central idea of a text and analyze its development over the course of the text; provide an objective summary of the text.	
RL.6.2	Determine a theme or central idea of a text and how it is conveyed through particular details; provide a summary of the text distinct from personal opinions or judgments.	
RL.5.2	Determine a theme of a story, drama, or poem from details in the text, including how characters in a story or drama respond to challenges or how the speaker in a poem reflects upon a topic; summarize the text.	Students *summarize* the plot of Antoine de Saint-Exupery's *The Little Prince* and then reflect on the *challenges* facing the *characters in the story* while employing those and other *details in the text* to discuss the value of inquisitiveness and exploration as a *theme of the story.*
RL.4.2	Determine a theme of a story, drama, or poem from details in the text; summarize the text.	
RL.3.2	Recount stories, including fables, folktales, and myths from diverse cultures; determine the central message, lesson, or moral and explain how it is conveyed through key details in the text.	
RL.2.2	Recount stories, including fables and folktales from diverse cultures, and determine their central message, lesson, or moral.	Students *read fables and folktales from diverse cultures* that represent various origin takes, such as Rudyard Kiplings' "How the Camel Got His Hump" and Natalie Babbitt's *The Search for Delicious*, and paraphrase *their central message, lesson or moral.*
RL.1.2	Retell stories, including key details, and demonstrate understanding of their central message or lesson.	Students *retell* Arnold Lobel's *Frog and Toad Together* while *demonstrating* their *understanding of a central message or lesson of the story* (e.g., how friends are able to solve problems together or how hard work pays off).
RL.K.2.	With prompting and support, retell familiar stories, including key details.	
	Source: CCSSI, 2010a.	Source: CCSSI, 2010b.

gradual cycling through repeated exposure to iterations of the same concepts and processes each year breaks complex learning expectations into manageable teaching and learning targets (Wiggs, 2011).

Notice also in the far right column of Exhibit 4.1 that the sample performance tasks included in Appendix B illustrate the concepts and skills (shown in italics) embedded within the performance task using text of sufficient complexity, quality, and range. This side-by-side view of both a learning progression and related sample assessment tasks using text of sufficient complexity provides a marvelous perspective from which to view the focus of teaching (the standards) and the application of learning (the assessment). Recall that effective feedback, then, becomes the fuel that advances student learning in the direction of each grade-specific standard and each college and career anchor standard.

CONNECTING FEEDBACK AND "UNWRAPPING" THE COMMON CORE STATE STANDARDS

Using the information provided in Exhibit 4.1, let's apply our knowledge of this CCSS learning progression, the assessment task, and effective feedback to a fifth-grade scenario in which the teacher and students are examining assessment results for **RL.5.2.** But first, it is critical to engage in the "unwrapping" the standards process to be able to clearly answer the first question of effective feedback: "Where is learning going?"

In the second chapter in this handbook, titled "Mapping Out the Learning Journey: 'Unwrapping' the Common Core State Standards," author Lisa Almeida provides step-by-step instructions for how to "unwrap" any standard. Almeida notes that "'unwrapping' the standards is a process that illuminates exactly what students are responsible for learning and what teachers are responsible for teaching."

"A powerful way educators can pinpoint the precise knowledge and skills contained in the wording of the standards is to 'unwrap' those standards. 'Unwrapping' means to analyze and deconstruct grade-level and course-specific standards for a unit of study to determine exactly what students need to know (concepts) and be able to do (skills). How each skill is applied to a particular concept determines its corresponding level of cognitive rigor. Determining the level of rigor in each skill is an important factor when later designing assessment questions and instruction to reflect that same degree of rigor" (Ainsworth, 2003).

By examining the "unwrapped" standard closely, it is easier for a fifth-grade teacher to discern *where learning is going* and the

BOOK FOUR EXHIBIT 4.2   **Illustration of an "Unwrapped" Standard**

RL.5.2: Determine a theme of a story, drama, or poem from details in the text, including how characters in a story or drama respond to challenges or how the speaker in a poem reflects upon a topic; summarize the text.	
Bloom's Level	**Skills and Concepts**
4	**DETERMINE** • a theme (from details in the text) • story (including how characters respond to challenges) • drama (including how characters respond to challenges) • poem (including how the speaker reflects upon a topic)
2	**SUMMARIZE** • the text

level of cognitive rigor expected. "Unwrapping" the standard provides the clear and vivid detail required for teachers to "pinpoint" the exact focus that will guide instructional planning and assessment design (see Exhibit 4.2). Notice also that when the sample performance task is lined up side-by-side with the "unwrapped" standard, as illustrated in Exhibit 4.3, it becomes even more apparent that only part of **RL.5.2** is addressed in the sample performance task.

A quick analysis of the "unwrapped" **RL.5.2** standard with analysis of the demands embedded in the performance task example is a useful exercise for both the fifth-grade teacher and students when they are making sense of assessment results. Per-

BOOK FOUR
EXHIBIT
4.3

"Unwrapped" Standard and Sample Performance Task

RL.5.2: Determine a theme of a story, drama, or poem from details in the text, including how characters in a story or drama respond to challenges or how the speaker in a poem reflects upon a topic; summarize the text.

Bloom's Levels	Skills and Concepts	Sample Performance Task
4	**DETERMINE** • **a theme (from details in the text)** • **story (including how characters respond to challenges)** • drama (including how characters respond to challenges) • poem (including how the speaker reflects upon a topic)	Students *summarize* the plot of Antoine de Saint-Exupery's *The Little Prince* and then reflect on the *challenges* facing the *characters in the story* while employing those and other *details in the text* to discuss the value of inquisitiveness and exploration as a *theme* of the *story.*
2	**SUMMARIZE** • **the text**	

Note: **Bolded** items in the *"unwrapped"* standard are represented with an equivalent task demand in the sample performance task.

spective on how the assessment task relates directly back to the details of the standard enables users of this information to more specifically answer the second question of effective feedback: "How am I doing?" Better yet, careful examination of the results of the assessment against the "unwrapped" standard will provide both the teacher and the students with detailed information about the components of **RL.5.2** for which the student has successfully demonstrated grade-level proficiency, which attributes of **RL.5.2** have not yet been mastered, and which aspects of **RL.5.2** the assessment did not address. Thus, the information gained from examining assessment-based results for this task not only provides useful feedback to both teachers and students relative to the student's current level of proficiency at this standard, but also provides useful feedback to *diagnose* future instructional adjustments. Future instructional adjustments can then be designed to address the third question of effective feedback: "Where should learning go next? Exactly what did the student do well on and exactly where does learning of this standard appear to break down?"

Future instructional adjustments for any given student will depend entirely on evidence gathered regarding what the student knows and is able to do in relation to the task demands outlined in each grade-specific standard. Exhibit 4.4 illustrates that when students demonstrate that they are already proficient on a given grade-specific standard (e.g., **RL.5.2**), one option is to provide challenge by accelerating students to the next set of grade-specific standards in the learning progression (in this case, **RL.6.2**). Similarly when students demonstrate that they are not yet proficient on a given grade-specific standard, one option is to revisit prior learning expectations articulated in earlier grade-specific standards (in this case, **RL.4.2**). Using evidence gained from

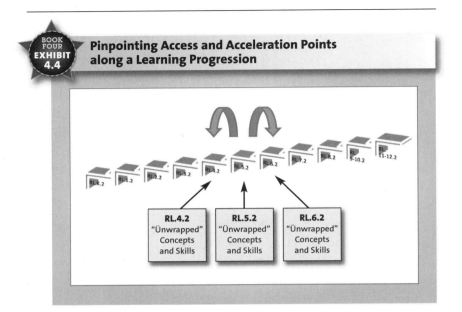

BOOK FOUR EXHIBIT 4.4

Pinpointing Access and Acceleration Points along a Learning Progression

assessment-based results, information about the learning progressions, and the level of rigor gleaned from "unwrapping" the concepts and skills within the standard, an astonishing degree of detail is provided to *diagnose* where learning ought to go next. In this way, the teacher is able to zoom in on specific, manageable instructional targets, coupled with "just right" feedback that provides the fuel for students to continue to advance along the building blocks in the learning pathways.

CONNECTING FEEDBACK AND THE PROFESSIONAL LEARNING COMMUNITIES/ DATA TEAMS PROCESS

While individual teachers and their students benefit from the detailed knowledge harvested from examining assessment-based results against the task demands of grade-specific standards, this same information works exceptionally well in the context of a Professional Learning Community and/or Data Team meeting. In fact, each author in this handbook on *Navigating Assessment and Collaboration with the Common Core State Standards* advocates for working together in collaborative partnerships to achieve the rigorous expectations outlined in the CCSS. Indeed, Professional Learning Communities and Data Teams are two highly developed formative structures ideally suited for advancing student achievement of the CCSS. In Chapter Three of this handbook, titled "Leveraging Data Teams and Professional Learning Communities for Success on the Common Core," author Laura Besser provides a detailed synthesis of how the Data Teams process is used to connect with the CCSS. Besser states that, "the Data Teams process provides the vehicle for the formative monitoring and evaluation that the CCSS require in order to measure formative growth of students." Data Teams, then, are a formal process for acquiring assessment-based evidence and using that information to provide feedback to advance learning.

Let's apply the principles discussed earlier to how Data Team members, together, might examine assessment results for standard **RL.5.2** and provide feedback to students on what comes next in the learning process. Exhibit 4.5 illustrates a hypothetical example of performance data collected for a fifth-grade team. As one ex-

Examining Assessment Results in a Data Team Meeting

Performance Data for RL.5.2: Students *summarize* the plot of Antoine de Saint-Exupery's *The Little Prince* and then reflect on the *challenges* facing the *characters in the story* while employing those and other *details in the text* to discuss the value of inquisitiveness and exploration as a *theme* of the *story*.

Teacher Names	Number of Students Assessed	Proficient		Not Yet Proficient		
		Number and Names of Students Far Above Proficiency	Number and Names of Students Who Meet Proficiency	Number and Names of Students Who Are Close to Proficiency	Number and Names of Students Who Have Far to Go	Number and Names of Students in Need of Extensive Support
Mr. Jones	26	2 Aubrie Zack	8 Caitlin Wade Barney Shane Lillian Jaime Wallace Maxine	10 Betsy Camilla Maddie Lois Kristen Perry Vaughn Seth Rhett Thomas	3 Faith Danielle Tab	3 Edena Ray Pablo
Mrs. Smith	27	3 Gayle Fatima Rick	10 Gabriella Daisy Libby Natalie Becky Toby Sam Rob Walker Patrick	9 Loren Hannah Ingrid Heather Peter Wayne Todd Ken Bjorn	3 Harriet Kallie Simon	2 Barbara Ulysses
Ms. Doe	27	5 Kendra Georgia Irene Kalb Vance	13 Lynne Carey Hallie Belinda Gina Carol Ophelia Wendell Serge Bryon Brad Travis Vernon	6 Candice Marcia Gilda Sanford Paul Ward	2 Kevin Xavier	1 Lucille
Total	80 (100%)	10 (12%)	31 (39%)	25 (31%)	8 (10%)	6 (8%)
		41 (51%)		39 (49%)		

Source: Adapted from Peery, 2011, p. 64.

amines the performance data for **RL.5.2** for this fifth-grade team, note how efficiently this one-page data display captures the number and names of students who are at various degrees of proficiency in mastering the assessed attributes of **RL.5.2**. At a glance, this data display addresses the following feedback questions: "Where is learning going?"; "How are fifth-grade students doing?"; and "How can we use the data to determine where learning might go next for each student in each performance band?"

As the fifth-grade Data Team responds to a series of explicit steps outlined in the Data Team meeting process, additional data are examined, inferences are generated, and needs are prioritized, all with the outcome of moving all students to mastery of each of the Common Core State Standards.

Glance back at Exhibit 4.1 illustrating the learning progression for reading for literature standard 2. One option, among several, for this Data Team to consider might be to utilize knowledge of the learning progressions to differentiate next steps for each of the five performance groups. Exhibit 4.6 outlines one possible use of the learning progressions to provide clear feedback to students on where they are in relation to the goal and what must happen now to close the gap between where the student is and where the student must go to move toward the ultimate goal of achieving college, career, and citizenship readiness.

BOOK FOUR EXHIBIT 4.6

Using Knowledge of the Learning Progressions and Performance Levels

The following is one illustration of how to use knowledge of a learning progression for reading for literature standard 2 to point the direction of instructional adjustments for students in each proficiency band based on performance data for **RL.5.2**.

Teacher Names	Number of Students Assessed	Proficient		Not Yet Proficient		
		Number and Names of Students Far Above Proficiency	Number and Names of Students Who Meet Proficiency	Number and Names of Students Who Are Close to Proficient	Number and Names of Students Who Have Far to Go	Number and Names of Students in Need of Extensive Support
Mr. Jones	26	**RL.7.2** Determine a theme or central idea of a text and analyze its development over the course of the text; provide an objective summary of the text.	**RL.5.2** Determine a theme of a story, drama, or poem from details in the text, including how characters in a story or drama respond to challenges or how the speaker in a poem reflects upon a topic; summarize the text.	**RL.4.2** Determine a theme of a story, drama, or poem from details in the text; summarize the text.	**RL.3.2** Recount stories, including fables, folktales, and myths from diverse cultures; determine the central message, lesson, or moral, and explain how it is conveyed through key details in the text.	**RL.1.2** Retell stories, including key details, and demonstrate understanding of their central message or lesson.
Mrs. Smith	27					
Ms. Doe	27					
Total	80 (100%)	10 (12%)	31 (39%)	25 (31%)	8 (10%)	6 (8%)
		41 (51%)		39 (49%)		

THE FINE ART OF GIVING FEEDBACK

This chapter has focused exclusively on exploring formative assessment structures that utilize feedback as central to supporting attainment of progressive student mastery on the grade-specific standards outlined in the Common Core State Standards. The fine art of actually delivering teacher feedback to students is beyond the scope of this chapter. However, rest assured that the process of "how" to deliver effective teacher feedback that is useful to the student's learning journey is well documented in a plethora of research studies, articles, and books on this topic. The following are three such examples:

In the book *Visible Learning* (2009), author John Hattie synthesizes the results of more than 800 meta-analyses relating to achievement, and states that "feedback was among the most powerful influences on achievement. Most programs that worked best were based on heavy dollops of feedback" (p. 173). He further outlines a four-part model for feedback consisting of feedback at the task level (how well tasks are understood or performed), feedback at the process level (the process needed to understand or perform tasks), feedback at the self-regulatory level (self-monitoring, directing, and regulating of actions), and feedback at the self level (personal evaluations, and effect). Hattie provides evidence from research that distinguishes effective from ineffective feedback and when it is better to provide elaborations through instruction than to provide feedback on poorly understood concepts. He notes that "feedback is not *the* answer to effective teaching and learning; rather it is one powerful answer" (p. 177).

In her book *How to Give Effective Feedback to Your Students* (2008), author Susan M. Brookhart synthesizes aspects of teacher feedback that research has identified as important. Throughout the book, she provides both a thorough discussion and specific examples regarding strategic choices that teachers make for feedback (timing, amount, mode, and audience) and the kinds of choices teachers make about the feedback content (focus, comparison, function, valence, clarity, specificity, and tone).

Anita L. Archer and Charles A. Hughes, in their book *Explicit Instruction: Effective and Efficient Teaching* (2011), provide a deep discussion and clear examples that summarize various types of feedback, including the finer points of delivering corrective feedback. They note, "In summary, good corrections are consistently and immediately provided, match the type of error made by the student, are specific in the information they convey, and focus on the correct response. In addition, corrections are delivered in an encouraging tone and end with the correct response" (p. 180).

SUMMARY

- Common formative assessment is most beneficial to teachers and students when *both* use the results

  - as feedback to determine current level of proficiency; and

  - as feedback to *diagnose* future instructional adjustments.

- The learning progressions embedded within the Common Core State Standards provide an ideal context for connecting effective feedback in the arena of common formative assessment to specifically answer questions about where learning is going and the status of the learner at any given point, and they provide an opportunity to clarify next steps along the learning pathway.

- Using evidence gained from assessment-based results, information about the learning progressions, and the level of rigor gleaned from "unwrapping" the concepts and skills within the standard, an astonishing degree of detail is available to provide precise feedback to students to keep learning moving forward.

- Professional Learning Communities and Data Teams are two highly developed formative structures ideally suited for providing specific feedback to advance student achievement of the CCSS for all performance groups.

- Effective feedback is the fuel that advances student learning in the direction of the hope and the promise of the Common Core State Standards.

References

Ainsworth, L. (2003). *"Unwrapping" the standards: A simple process to make standards manageable.* Englewood, CO: Lead + Learn Press.

Ainsworth, L. (2007). Common formative assessments: The centerpiece of an integrated standards-based assessment system. In *Ahead of the curve: The power of assessment to transform teaching and learning.* Bloomington, IN: Solution Tree Press.

Archer, A. L., & Hughes, C. A. (2011). *Explicit instruction: Effective and efficient teaching.* New York: The Guilford Press.

Brookhart, S. M. (2008). *How to give effective feedback to your students.* Alexandria, VA: ASCD.

Common Core State Standards Initiative (CCSSI). (2010a). *Common Core State Standards for English language arts & literacy in history/social studies, science, and technical subjects* (PDF document). Retrieved from www.corestandards.org/assets/CCSSI_ELA%20Standards.pdf

Common Core State Standards Initiative (CCSSI). (2010b). *Common Core State Standards for English language arts & literacy in history/social studies, science, and technical subjects: Appendix B.* Retrieved from www.corestandards.org/assets/Appendix_B.pdf

Hattie, J. C. (2009). *Visible learning: A synthesis of over 800 meta-analyses relating to achievement.* New York: Routledge.

Hattie, J., & Timperley, H. (2007). The power of feedback. *Review of Educational Research, 77*(1), 81–112.

Peery, A. (2011). *The data teams experience: A guide for effective meetings.* Englewood, CO: Lead + Learn Press.

Wiggs, M. (2011). Getting to know the Common Core State Standards. In *Standards and assessment: The core of quality instruction.* Englewood, CO: Lead + Learn Press.

Looking Ahead to Large-Scale Assessment of the Common Core State Standards

Derek C. Briggs

The large-scale multistate assessment consortia that are the subject of this chapter can be thought of as the offspring of two well-intentioned parents: the Common Core State Standards Initiative (coordinated by the National Governors Association Center for Best Practices and the Council of Chief State School Officers) and the Race to the Top (RTTP) grant competition (sponsored by the United States Department of Education). Without the impetus of a shared understanding of what students should know and be able to do as they advance from preschool through high school, it would be impossible to envision a single standardized assessment that could be administered to students across different states. Without the challenge (and the funding) from the federal government to develop a system of assessment capable of measuring that which has proven difficult to measure in the past—complex thinking and problem solving—it would be impossible to leverage the resources needed to envision, design, and implement a novel and innovative large-scale assessment infrastructure that will test students on the concepts and skills embedded in the Common Core State Standards.

The infrastructure in question is being developed through the efforts of four different consortia that were funded through the RTTP grants: the Partnership for Assessment of Readiness for College and Careers (PARCC), the SMARTER Balanced Assessment Consortium (SBAC), the National Center and State Collaborative Partnership, and the Dynamic Learning Maps consortium. The PARCC and SBAC consortia are responsible for designing computer-based tests to be administered to the general population of students; the National Center and State Collaborative Partnership and Dynamic Learning Maps consortia have as their focus the development of alternative assessments for students with significant cognitive disabilities. The assessment systems from all four consortia are expected to go "live" as of the 2014–15 school year. In this chapter, I focus attention on the assessment systems being designed by PARCC and SBAC*.

PARTNERSHIP FOR ASSESSMENT OF READINESS FOR COLLEGE AND CAREERS

As described on the PARCC Web site (www.parcconline.org/about -parcc), PARCC's goal is to create "a common set of K–12 assessments in English and math anchored in what it takes to be ready for college and careers. These new K–12 assessments will build a pathway to college and career readiness by the end of high school, mark students' progress toward this goal from third grade up, and provide teachers with timely information to inform instruction

---

* This is in no way to diminish the critical importance of the work being done to assess students with significant cognitive disabilities, but to do these efforts justice is outside the scope of this chapter.

and provide student support." There are 24 states that are members of PARCC, and 18 of those states are governing members (in bold): Alabama, **Arizona, Arkansas,** Colorado, **District of Columbia, Florida, Georgia, Illinois, Indiana,** Kentucky, **Louisiana, Maryland, Massachusetts, Mississippi, New Jersey, New Mexico, New York,** North Dakota, **Ohio, Oklahoma,** Pennsylvania, **Rhode Island,** South Carolina and **Tennessee.** To become a governing member, a state must agree that it will exclusively administer the PARCC assessment system to its general population of students as of 2014–15. Governing states play a key role in providing input with regard to PARCC's policy and operational decisions, and each state has a liaison on PARCC's leadership team.

The PARCC assessment system will include four components: 1) a diagnostic assessment to be administered at the beginning of the school year; 2) a midyear assessment that should be predictive of a student's likely performance by the end of the school year; 3) a performance-based assessment in the last quarter of the school year; and 4) an end-of-year summative assessment. The diagnostic and midyear assessments will be optional and at the discretion of a state or school district to administer; the performance-based and end-of-year assessments will be mandatory for all states using the PARCC system. All of these components will be available for students in grades 3–11.

SMARTER BALANCED ASSESSMENT CONSORTIUM

The goal of SBAC is to develop assessments that are "valid, support and inform instruction, provide accurate information about what students know and can do, and measure student achievement against standards designed to ensure that all students gain the knowledge and skills needed to succeed in college and the workplace" (www.k12.wa.us/smarter/faq.aspx). There are 28 states that are members of SBAC, 21 of which are governing members (in bold): Alabama, **California**, Colorado, **Connecticut**, **Delaware**, **Hawaii**, **Idaho**, **Iowa**, **Kansas**, Kentucky, **Maine**, **Michigan**, **Missouri**, **Montana**, **Nevada**, **New Hampshire**, **North Carolina**, North Dakota, **Oregon**, Pennsylvania, South Carolina, **South Dakota**, **Utah**, **Vermont**, **Washington**, **West Virginia**, **Wisconsin**, and Wyoming. Governing states play the same role in SBAC as they do in PARCC. Nongoverning states are those that are "advisory" members of both consortia; eventually, these states will have to choose to join one or neither of the consortia. There are five states that have already chosen not to participate with either PARCC or SBAC: Alaska, Minnesota, Nebraska, Texas, and Virginia. Exhibit 5.1 shows a summary of state affiliations with PARCC and SBAC.

The SBAC assessment system includes three major components: 1) a computer-adaptive summative assessment that will be administered during the last 12 weeks of the school year; 2) interim assessments that can be used to predict student performance on the summative assessment while also providing feedback on student progress; and 3) formative assessment resources to help teachers diagnose and respond to the needs of their students as they teach the content of the CCSS. Like PARCC, the use and timing of the formative and interim components will be optional, while participation in the summative component will be mandatory. Like PARCC, performance-based tasks are a key element of their planned assessments, but SBAC views performance-based tasks as one of many different item formats that will be embedded within their summative end-of-year assessment.

BOOK FOUR EXHIBIT 5.1

State Affiliations with Large-Scale Assessment Consortia as of December 2011

State	PARCC	SBAC
Alabama	X	X
Alaska		
Arizona	X	
Arkansas	X	
California		X
Colorado	X	X
Connecticut		X
Delaware		X
District of Columbia	X	
Florida	X	
Georgia	X	
Hawaii		X
Idaho		X
Illinois	X	
Indiana	X	
Iowa		X
Kansas		X
Kentucky	X	X
Louisiana	X	
Maine		X
Maryland	X	
Massachusetts	X	
Michigan		X
Minnesota		
Mississippi	X	
Missouri		X
Montana		X
Nebraska		
Nevada		X
New Hampshire		X
New Jersey	X	
New Mexico	X	
New York	X	
North Carolina		X
North Dakota	X	X
Ohio	X	
Oklahoma	X	
Oregon		X
Pennsylvania	X	X
Rhode Island	X	
South Carolina	X	X
South Dakota		X
Tennessee	X	
Texas		
Utah		X
Vermont		X
Virginia		
Washington		X
West Virginia		X
Wisconsin		X
Wyoming		X

DISTINCTIONS BETWEEN PARCC AND SBAC

In general, there are far more similarities between the two consortia than there are differences. SBAC has generally been perceived as placing a greater emphasis on balancing summative and formative assessment uses within its planned system (Darling-Hammond and Pecheone, 2010) while PARCC, because it is being managed by the organization Achieve, has been perceived as placing a greater emphasis on first and foremost establishing a rigorous basis for summative accountability. However, the planned mixes of formative and summative components that each consortium is developing are, at this point in the process, indistinguishable. It remains to be seen how the substance of these components will differ once they have been fully designed and implemented.

There are, however, two important structural differences between the two planned assessment systems. First, while both PARCC and SBAC will be administering their assessments on computers, only SBAC has committed itself to a purely computer-adaptive assessment. What this means is that when a student takes an SBAC test during the 2014–15 school year, the difficulty of each item the student is administered will depend on how the student has responded to the previous item that was administered. If it works as intended, a computer-adaptive test is a very efficient way to assess students, because it will generally take less time to hone in on a student's ability level when compared with a test in which a fixed set of items is administered, as will be the case for PARCC. A major advantage of a computer-adaptive test is that it allows for on-the-fly score reporting, which facilitates immediate feedback of results to students and teachers. A drawback to the computer-adaptive testing approach is that it places a heavy weight on establishing a large item "bank" (in this case, "large" means *thousands* of items) before the assessment has been administered operationally. It can be challenging to unequivocally establish the validity of the items in this bank ahead of time, and once the assessment goes live, it is hard to make major adjustments to the system while maintaining comparability with previous results.

A second important distinction is that PARCC is planning grade-specific end-of-year summative assessments for grades 3–11; as of this writing, SBAC was only planning to develop summative assessments for grades 3–8 and 11.

WHAT CAN WE EXPECT FROM THE PARCC AND SBAC ASSESSMENTS IN 2014?

The assessment systems under design in each of the multistate consortia are currently still at the blueprint stage. What is known with certainty about the assessment systems that will emerge is limited, but in a general sense the ambitions are clear:

1. Tests will be administered to students on computers.

2. Test items will be written such that they are aligned to the subject-specific knowledge and skills described in the CCSS.

3. The tests will contain novel item formats (e.g., performance-based tasks, technology-enhanced items) crafted to better assess not just what students *know* but also what they can *do*.

4. The tests will be designed so that they can be used not only to assess where students are at any one point in

time, but also to assess how much they have grown, and the extent to which they are on track to be adequately prepared to start college or a career upon graduation from high school.

5. In addition to an end-of-year assessment, the full assessment system will include formative and interim test materials intended to help teachers (and parents) better understand the academic strengths and weaknesses of students throughout the academic school year, and, if necessary, take action through targeted interventions before the year is over.

Not only are these ambitions lofty, but each one represents a departure from the way that large-scale assessments have been designed, administered, and used over the past decade under the auspices of the No Child Left Behind Act of 2001. Fulfilling all these ambitions by 2014 will be a major challenge for each consortium. The logistics of shifting testing systems that, for most states, have been administered on paper and pencil, to one that is administered solely on computers is in and of itself daunting. However, I want to focus on three reasons why the assessment systems that will emerge from the consortia are likely to represent an improvement over the state-specific systems they will be replacing. The first is that the leadership teams guiding each of the consortia are following assessment design principles that, if well implemented, should result in greater coherence and clarity vis-à-vis the interpretations that can be supported by a child's test score. The second is that the CCSS, to which the new tests are to be aligned, promote new ways of conceptualizing and interpreting growth in student achievement. The third is that all the consortia are committed to the development and use of performance tasks and innovative technology-enhanced items as a means of assessing the sorts of higher-order thinking skills that students are expected to master, but which have been difficult to measure in the past.

EVIDENCE-CENTERED DESIGN

Both the PARCC and SBAC assessment systems are using an approach known as "evidence-centered design" (Mislevy and Riconscente, 2006; National Research Council, 2001) to build their testing "blueprints." An example of an evidence-centered design (ECD) template is provided in Exhibit 5.2. The ECD approach begins by first operationalizing *claims* about the knowledge, skills, and abilities (KSAs) that students are expected to master. In the second step, the *evidence* that would be necessary to support such claims is specified. In the third step, *tasks* or *items* are written in order to elicit this evidence. The ECD approach is consistent with contemporary developments in test validation theory (Kane, 2006) because it builds an argument about score interpretations that can be falsified if it could be established that there is a broken link in the hypothesized connection between items, evidence, and claims.

Exhibits 5.3 and 5.4 compare the ECD claims that have been proposed for the English language arts and mathematics assessments being developed by PARCC and SBAC, respectively. It is interesting to note that even though the two consortia have been working independently, because each group has taken the CCSS as its starting point, the substance of the claims being made by each are remarkably similar.

BOOK FOUR EXHIBIT 5.2

Example of an Evidence-Centered Design Template for Item Development

ECD Element	Feature	Definition
Claim What combination of student knowledge, skills, and abilities (KSAs) is being assessed?	**Focal KSAs**	Primary KSAs targeted by this design pattern
Evidence What evidence or observations is/are needed?	**Potential Observations**	Observed behaviors of students that can provide evidence with regard to understanding of Focal KSAs
	Potential Work Products	What students say, do, or make that provides evidence about the Focal KSAs
	Potential Rubrics	Some evaluation techniques that may apply
Items/Tasks What tasks should elicit that evidence?	**Characteristic Features**	Aspects of assessment situations likely to evoke the desired evidence
	Variable Features	Aspects of assessment situations that can be varied in order to control difficulty or target emphasis on various aspects of KSAs or provide support for additional KSAs

BOOK FOUR EXHIBIT 5.3

Evidence-Centered Design Claims for English Language Arts: PARCC and SBAC

PARCC Draft (December 2011)	SBAC Draft (September 2011)
Claim 1: Students read and comprehend a range of sufficiently complex texts independently. **Subclaim 1.1:** Students draw evidence from reading of grade-level, complex literary text. **Subclaim 1.2:** Students draw evidence from reading of grade-level, complex informational text. **Subclaim 1.3:** Students use context to determine the meaning of words and phrases. **Claim 2:** Students write effectively when using and/or analyzing sources. **Subclaim 2.1:** Students produce clear and coherent writing in which the development, organization, and style are appropriate to the task, purpose, and audience. **Subclaim 2.2:** Students demonstrate knowledge of conventions and other important elements of language. **Claim 3** (for grades 6–11)**:** Students build and present knowledge through research and the integration, comparison, and synthesis of ideas.	**Claim 1:** Students can read closely and critically to comprehend a range of increasingly complex literary and informational texts. **Claim 2:** Students can produce effective writing for a range of purposes and audiences. **Claim 3:** Students can employ effective speaking and listening skills for a range of purposes and audiences. **Claim 4:** Students can engage appropriately in collaborative and independent inquiry to investigate/research topics, pose questions, and gather and present information. **Claim 5:** Students can skillfully use and interpret written language across a range of literacy tasks.

Evidence-Centered Design Claims for Mathematics: PARCC and SBAC

PARCC Draft (December 2011)	SBAC Draft (December 2011)
Claim: The student solves grade-level/course-level problems in mathematics as set forth in the Standards for Mathematical Content with connections to the Standards for Mathematical Practice.	**Claim 1**: Students can explain and apply mathematical concepts and interpret and carry out mathematical procedures with precision and fluency.
Subclaim 1: The student solves problems involving the *Major Content* highlighted for her grade/course with connections to the Standards for Mathematical Practice.	**Claim 2**: Students can solve a range of complex well-posed problems in pure and applied mathematics, making productive use of knowledge and problem-solving strategies.
Subclaim 2: The student solves problems involving the *Additional and Supporting Content* for her grade/course with connections to the Standards for Mathematical Practice.	**Claim 3**: Students can clearly and precisely construct viable arguments to support their own reasoning and to critique the reasoning of others.
Subclaim 3: The student expresses appropriate *mathematical reasoning* by constructing viable arguments, critiquing the reasoning of others, and/or attending to precision when making mathematical statements.	**Claim 4**: Students can analyze complex, real-world scenarios and can construct and use mathematical models to interpret and solve problems.
Subclaim 4: The student *solves real-world problems* with a degree of difficulty appropriate to the grade/course by applying knowledge and skills articulated in the standards for the current grade/course.	
Subclaim 5: The student *demonstrates fluency* as set forth in the Standards for Mathematical Content in her grade.	

GROWTH AND LEARNING PROGRESSIONS

The assessment systems being contemplated by the consortia will offer a potentially novel way to conceptualize across grade growth in achievement. Exhibit 5.5 shows two different interpretations associated with two distinct, though not mutually exclusive, growth conceptualizations. The left side of Exhibit 5.5 contains planes that represent a subject area (e.g., mathematics) at a given grade level (e.g., grade 3). Within each plane are light-colored shapes, and within each shape is a series of dots. The shapes are meant to represent different "content domains" (e.g., numerical operations, measurement & data, geometry); the dots represent domain-specific performance standards that delineate grade-level expectations for students (e.g., within the domain of measurement & data: "Generate measurement data by measuring lengths using rulers marked with halves and fourths of an inch"). This sort of taxonomy has traditionally been used to deconstruct the often amorphous notion of "mathematics achievement" into the discrete KSAs that should, in principle, be teachable within a grade-level curriculum. Such an approach facilitates the design of grade-specific assessments because test items can be written to correspond to specific statements about what students should know and be able to do. I refer to the assessment design implied by the left side of Exhibit 5.5 as the "domain-sampling" approach.

When assessments are developed according to a domain-sampling approach, the intent is for growth to be interpreted as the extent to which a student has demonstrated increased mastery of the different domains that comprise mathematical ability. This is indicated by the single arrow showing movement from the plane for a lower grade to the plane for a higher grade. For exam-

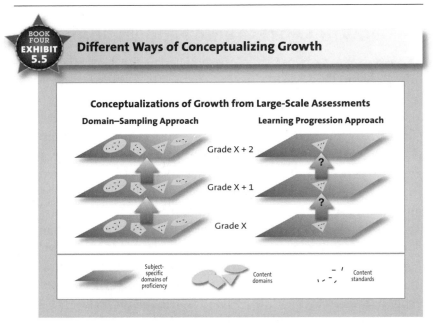

BOOK
FOUR
EXHIBIT
5.5

Different Ways of Conceptualizing Growth

Conceptualizations of Growth from Large-Scale Assessments

Domain–Sampling Approach   Learning Progression Approach

Grade X + 2

Grade X + 1

Grade X

Subject-
specific
domains of
proficiency

Content
domains

Content
standards

ple, according to the CCSS, a composite of mathematics achieve-ment could be defined from grade to grade as a function of five content domains and six skills domains. A drawback to this approach is that if both the domains and the content specifications within each plane change considerably from grade to grade, then it becomes possible for students to appear to "grow" even if distinct content is tested across years.

A different basis for a growth conceptualization comes from what I refer to as the *learning progression* approach. Learning progressions have been defined as empirically grounded and testable hypotheses about how students' understanding of core concepts within a subject domain grows and becomes more sophisticated over time with appropriate instruction (Corcoran, Mosher, and

Rogat, 2009). The key idea shown in the right panel of Exhibit 5.5 is the presence of an implicit *hypothesis* about the nature of growth: the way that students' understanding of some core concept or concepts *within the same domain* is expected to become qualitatively more sophisticated from grade to grade. The notion that this constitutes a hypothesis about growth to be tested empirically is represented by the question marks placed on the arrows that link one grade to the next. The learning progression approach to growth values the assessment of depth of knowledge within a single domain over the assessment of breadth of knowledge across multiple domains.

Both of these conceptualizations of growth might, in principle, be supported by the tests that will be developed for PARCC and SBAC. What is exciting about the potential for a learning progression growth interpretation is that this could lead to assessment results that are much more diagnostically useful than anything that has been seen in the past.

PERFORMANCE TASKS AND USE OF TECHNOLOGY

Messick (1996) defined a performance assessment as something that requires a student to "perform, create, or produce something over a sufficient duration of time to permit evaluation of either the process or the product, or both." A prominent feature of the initial SBAC and PARCC proposals was the promise for an increased emphasis on performance-based assessment.

> The Partnership will develop challenging performance tasks
> and innovative, computer-enhanced items that elicit

complex demonstrations of learning and measure the full range of knowledge and skills necessary to succeed in college and 21st-century careers. They will send a strong, clear signal to educators about the kinds of instruction and types of performances needed for students to demonstrate college and career readiness. (PARCC)

The commitment of the Consortium to the use of performance events will be central to our ability to measure student knowledge and skills against the full range of the college- and career-ready standards. The performance components will reflect more ambitious events that can measure aspects of student performance that are reflected in the [Common Core State Standards] but have traditionally been difficult to measure on standardized assessments, including skills such as the use of relevant evidence and technology, thoughtful critique, and adaptive reasoning. Student performance on the adaptive summative assessment will be combined with the performance measures to provide the accurate measure of student achievement. (SBAC)

Performance tasks have long been viewed as a desirable alternative to more traditional short answer and multiple-choice item formats because they assess complex aspects of student reasoning and problem solving, which presumably cannot be adequately assessed via traditional item formats, and they provide a "signal" or "model" to teachers about desired instructional practices (Haertel, 1999; Linn, Baker, and Dunbar, 1991). The performance tasks being planned by each consortium are still in the early design stages, but what we know at this point is that they will almost surely involve multiple stages in which students are given a motivating prompt (i.e., reading passage, video clip, computer simulation) and then expected to compare and contrast, analyze, summarize, synthesize, and communicate their findings in writing.

A complement to these performance tasks will be the presumed availability of "technology-enhanced" items that make it possible to ask questions that are more engaging and interactive than the static items to which students have become accustomed on traditional pencil-and-paper assessments. Both PARCC and SBAC are hoping that the use of innovations in computer-based technology will help to increase the motivation of students to give their best efforts while being assessed. Furthermore, the use of a more flexible testing environment should make it easier to develop accommodations for students who are English language learners or have special needs. The flip side, of course, is that both consortia will need to anticipate some bumpiness as schools and their students make the transition from the paper-and-pencil test format to the computer-based test format. For younger children in particular, computers can be motivating in the wrong way if they become distracted by features such as highlighting text, or clicking certain buttons.

SUMMARY

The design and development of a novel and innovative assessment system by two multistate assessment consortia is well under way. By the 2014–15 school year, American students in all but a handful of states will be taking assessments that are computer-based and aligned to the CCSS. The assessments will include both formative and summative components, each of which will have been crafted according to the principles of evidence-centered design. This should make the intended claims that test scores can support more transparent and easier communication to parents. Unlike the previous generation of large-scale assessments spawned by No Child Left Behind, the PARCC and SBAC assessments will place a much greater emphasis on the growth of student achievement over time. Finally, the new assessments will include a greater emphasis on the higher-order thinking skills that students will be expected to demonstrate in their responses to performance-based tasks and technology-enhanced items.

References

Corcoran, T., Mosher, F. A., & Rogat, A. (2009). *Learning progressions in science: An evidence-based approach to reform* (CPRE Research Report #RR-63). Retrieved June 15, 2009, from www.cpre.org/images/stories/cpre_ pdfs/lp_science_rr63.pdf

Darling-Hammond, L., & Pecheone, R. (2010). *Developing an internationally comparable balanced assessment system that supports high-quality learning.* Presented at the National Conference on Next Generation K–12 Assessment Systems, Center for K–12 Assessment & Performance Management with the Education Commission of the States (ECS) and the Council of Great City Schools (CGCS), Washington, DC.

Haertel, E. H. (1999). Performance assessment and education reform. *Phi Delta Kappan, 80,* 662–666.

Kane, M. (2006). Validation. In R. L. Brennan (Ed.), *Educational measurement* (4th ed.) (pp. 17–64). Westport, CT: American Council on Education/Praeger.

Linn, R. L., Baker, E. L., & Dunbar, S. B. (1991). Complex, performance-based assessment: Expectations and validation criteria. *Educational Researcher, 20*(8), 15.

Messick, S. (1996). Validity of performance assessments. In *Technical issues in large-scale performance assessment* (pp. 1–18). National Center for Education Statistics.

Mislevy, R. J., & Riconscente, M. M. (2006). Evidence-centered assessment design: Layers, concepts, and terminology. In S. Downing & T. Haladyna (Eds.), *Handbook of test development.* Mahwah, NJ: Erlbaum.

National Research Council (NRC). (2001). *Knowing what students know: The science and design of educational assessment.* J. Pellegrino, N. Chudowsky & R. Glaser (Eds.). Committee on the Foundations of Assessment. Washington, DC: National Academies Press.

Partnership for Assessment of Readiness for College and Careers (PARCC). www.parcconline.org/about-parcc

SMARTER Balanced Assessment Consortium (SBAC). www.k12.wa.us/smarter/

Index

Acceleration/access points, pinpointing, 90 (exh.)
Achievement, 38, 61, 67, 77, 82, 97, 111, 112, 116
measuring, 101–102, 114
Ahead of the Curve (Ainsworth), 25, 82–83
Ainsworth, Larry, 33, 49, 83
Almeida, Lisa, 86
Archer, Anita L., 96
Assessments, 18, 26, 28, 39, 86, 88, 89, 99, 111, 115–116
adjustments for, 1, 105
administering/scoring, 7, 75–76, 77
analyzing, 64
connecting, 2–5
creating, 7, 27, 30, 61
Data Teams and, 59, 60–61, 78, 92 (exh.)
effective, 29
end-of-unit, 5, 18
end-of-year, 101, 102, 105, 106
grade-specific, 111
high-stakes, 26, 57, 106
instruction and, 5–8
performance-based, 20, 110, 113
pre-/post-, 4, 38, 61, 75
results of, 6, 88
standardized, 99, 114
summative, 9, 102
using, 5–8

Besser, Laura, 76, 91
Big Ideas, 42 (exh.), 45, 46
determining, 10, 11, 13–15, 29
Essential Questions and, 16 (exh.), 24–25, 37
scoring guide for, 25 (exh.)
student directions for, 24 (exh.)
Bloom's Revised Taxonomy (Anderson and Krathwohl), 4, 13, 18, 21
Brookhart, Susan M.: on feedback, 95–96

Cognitive thinking, 6, 13, 36, 59
Collaboration, 26, 37, 38, 54, 55, 70, 77, 78

College and career readiness (CCR), 81, 84, 93, 106, 114
Common Core State Standards (CCSS), 2, 3, 29, 36, 38, 49, 53, 77, 84, 93, 95, 96, 105, 106
connection to, 55
design/organizational features of, 50, 81–82
grade-specific, 82
matching priority, 10, 11–12
promise of, 97
rigor of, 61
sample minutes, 71–72 (exh.)
steps for, 39
understanding, 21, 26
unwrapping, 10, 86–90
Common formative assessments (CFAs), 2, 7, 11, 26, 63, 65, 96
described, 8–10
designing, 10–25, 27–30
feedback and, 82–84, 86
summative assessments and, 9
using, 25–26, 30, 83
Common summative assessments (CSAs), 8, 9
Concepts, 12, 33, 38, 42 (exh.), 58, 66, 75, 97, 99
"unwrapping," 4, 13, 14–15, 14 (exh.), 16, 18, 29
"Connecting Common Core State Standards with Common Formative Assessments" (Ainsworth), 82
Constructed-response items, 7, 10, 24
described, 6
scoring guides for, 11, 21, 21 (exh.), 23 (exh.), 29
selected-response items and, 18, 20
writing, 10, 18, 19 (exh.), 20, 22 (exh.), 29
Council of Chief State School Officers, 99
Curriculum, 1, 2–5

Data, 53, 77, 111
assessment, 57

119